MznLnx

Missing Links Exam Preps

Exam Prep for

Finite Mathematics An Applied Approach

Sullivan, Mizrahi, 9th Edition

The MznLnx Exam Prep is your link from the texbook and lecture to your exams.
The MznLnx Exam Preps are unauthorized and comprehensive reviews of your textbooks.

All material provided by MznLnx and Rico Publications (c) 2010
Textbook publishers and textbook authors do not particpate in or contribute to these reviews.

MznLnx

Rico Publications

Exam Prep for Finite Mathematics An Applied Approach
9th Edition
Sullivan, Mizrahi

Publisher: Raymond Houge
Assistant Editor: Michael Rouger
Text and Cover Designer: Lisa Buckner
Marketing Manager: Sara Swagger
Project Manager, Editorial Production: Jerry Emerson
Art Director: Vernon Lowerui

Product Manager: Dave Mason
Editorial Assitant: Rachel Guzmanji
Pedagogy: Debra Long
Cover Image: Jim Reed/Getty Images
Text and Cover Printer: City Printing, Inc.
Compositor: Media Mix, Inc.

(c) 2010 Rico Publications
ALL RIGHTS RESERVED. No part of this work covered by the copyright may be reproduced or used in any form or by an means--graphic, electronic, or mechanical, including photocopying, recording, taping, Web distribution, information storage, and retrieval systems, or in any other manner--without the written permission of the publisher.

For more information about our products, contact us at:
Dave.Mason@RicoPublications.com

For permission to use material from this text or product, submit a request online to:
Dave.Mason@RicoPublications.com

Printed in the United States
ISBN:

Contents

CHAPTER 1
LINEAR EQUATIONS — 1

CHAPTER 2
SYSTEMS OF LINEAR EQUATIONS; MATRICES — 15

CHAPTER 3
LINEAR PROGRAMMING: GEOMETRIC APPROACH — 29

CHAPTER 4
LINEAR PROGRAMMING: SIMPLEX METHOD — 32

CHAPTER 5
FINANCE — 40

CHAPTER 6
SETS; COUNTING TECHNIQUES — 43

CHAPTER 7
PROBABILITY — 53

CHAPTER 8
ADDITIONAL PROBABILITY Topics — 59

CHAPTER 9
STATISTICS — 66

CHAPTER 10
MARKOV CHAINS; GAMES — 80

CHAPTER 11
LOGIC — 87

ANSWER KEY — 104

TO THE STUDENT

COMPREHENSIVE

The *MznLnx* Exam Prep series is designed to help you pass your exams. Editors at MznLnx review your textbooks and then prepare these practice exams to help you master the textbook material. Unlike study guides, workbooks, and practice tests provided by the texbook publisher and textbook authors, *MznLnx* gives you **all** of the material in each chapter in exam form, not just samples, so you can be sure to nail your exam.

MECHANICAL

The MznLnx Exam Prep series creates exams that will help you learn the subject matter as well as test you on your understanding. Each question is designed to help you master the concept. Just working through the exams, you gain an understanding of the subject--its a simple mechanical process that produces success.

INTEGRATED STUDY GUIDE AND REVIEW

MznLnx is not just a set of exams designed to test you, its also a comprehensive review of the subject content. Each exam question is also a review of the concept, making sure that you will get the answer correct without having to go to other sources of material. You learn as you go! Its the easiest way to pass an exam.

HUMOR

Studying can be tedious and dry. MznLnx's instructional design includes moderate humor within the exam questions on occassion, to break the tedium and revitalize the brain

Chapter 1. LINEAR EQUATIONS

1. In mathematics, the _____ of a Euclidean space is a special point, usually denoted by the letter O, used as a fixed point of reference for the geometry of the surrounding space. In a Cartesian coordinate system, the _____ is the point where the axes of the system intersect. In Euclidean geometry, the _____ may be chosen freely as any convenient point of reference.
    a. Interval
    b. OMAC
    c. Origin
    d. Autonomous system

2. In mathematics, a _____ can mean either an element of the set {1, 2, 3, ...} (i.e the positive integers) or an element of the set {0, 1, 2, 3, ...} (i.e. the non-negative integers).
    a. Bounded
    b. Degrees of freedom
    c. FISH
    d. Whole number

3. The _____ is the horizontal axis of a two- dimensional plot in the Cartesian coordinate system, that is typically pointed to the right. Also known as a right-handed coordinate system.
    a. 1-center problem
    b. X-axis
    c. 2-3 heap
    d. 120-cell

4. In reference to a 2D and 3D plane, the _____ is the vertical height of a 2D or 3D object.
    a. 1-center problem
    b. Y-axis
    c. 2-3 heap
    d. 120-cell

5. A _____ is an algebraic equation in which each term is either a constant or the product of a constant and a single variable. _____s can have one, two, three or more variables.

_____s occur with great regularity in applied mathematics.

a. Quartic equation
b. Quadratic equation
c. Linear equation
d. Difference of two squares

6. In quantum field theory and statistical mechanics in the thermodynamic limit, a system with a global symmetry can have more than one phase. For parameters where the symmetry is spontaneously broken, the system is said to be _____. When the global symmetry is unbroken the system is disordered.
    a. Ursell function
    b. Ordered
    c. Einstein relation
    d. Isoenthalpic-isobaric ensemble

7. In mathematics, an _____ is a collection of objects having two coordinates (or entries or projections), such that one can always uniquely determine the object, which is the first coordinate (or first entry or left projection) of the pair as well as the second coordinate (or second entry or right projection.) If the first coordinate is a and the second is b, the usual notation for an _____ is (a, b.) The pair is 'ordered' in that (a, b) differs from (b, a) unless a = b.
    a. Ordered pair
    b. A chemical equation
    c. A posteriori
    d. A Mathematical Theory of Communication

8. A _____ consists of one quarter of the coordinate plane.
    a. 2-3 heap
    b. 1-center problem
    c. Quadrant
    d. 120-cell

9. A _____ is a software program that facilitates symbolic mathematics. The core functionality of a CAS is manipulation of mathematical expressions in symbolic form.

Chapter 1. LINEAR EQUATIONS

The symbolic manipulations supported typically include

- simplification to the smallest possible expression or some standard form, including automatic simplification with assumptions and simplification with constraints
- substitution of symbolic, functors or numeric values for expressions
- change of form of expressions: expanding products and powers, partial and full factorization, rewriting as partial fractions, constraint satisfaction, rewriting trigonometric functions as exponentials, etc.
- partial and total differentiation
- symbolic constrained and unconstrained global optimization
- solution of linear and some non-linear equations over various domains
- solution of some differential and difference equations
- taking some limits
- some indefinite and definite integration, including multidimensional integrals
- integral transforms
- arbitrary-precision numeric operations
- Series operations such as expansion, summation and products
- matrix operations including products, inverses, etc.
- display of mathematical expressions in two-dimensional mathematical form, often using typesetting systems similar to TeX
- add-ons for use in applied mathematics such as physics packages for physical computation
- plotting graphs and parametric plots of functions in two and three dimensions, and animating them
- APIs for linking it on an external program such as a database, or using in a programming language to use the _____
- drawing charts and diagrams
- string manipulation such as matching and searching
- statistical computation
- Theorem proving and verification
- graphic production and editing such as CGI and signal processing as image processing
- sound synthesis

Many also include a programming language, allowing users to implement their own algorithms.

Some _____s focus on a specific area of application; these are typically developed in academia and are free.

   a. 1-center problem
   b. Computer algebra system
   c. 2-3 heap
   d. 120-cell

10.   In economics, specifically cost accounting, the _____ is the point at which cost or expenses and revenue are equal: there is no net loss or gain, and one has 'broken even'. Therefore has not made a profit or a loss.

Chapter 1. LINEAR EQUATIONS

In the linear Cost-Volume-Profit Analysis model, the _____ can be directly computed in terms of Total Revenue and Total Costs as:

$$TR = TC$$
$$P \times X = TFC + V \times X$$
$$P \times X - V \times X = TFC$$
$$(P - V) \times X = TFC$$
$$X = \frac{TFC}{P - V}$$

where:

- TFC is Total Fixed Costs,
- P is Unit Sale Price, and
- V is Unit Variable Cost.

The _____ can alternatively be computed as the point where Contribution equals Fixed Costs.

The quantity $(P - V)$ is of interest in its own right, and is called the Unit Contribution Margin: it is the marginal profit per unit, or alternatively the portion of each sale that contributes to Fixed Costs. Thus the _____ can be more simply computed as the point where Total Contribution = Total Fixed Cost:

$$\text{Total Contribution} = \text{Total Fixed Costs}$$
$$\text{Unit Contribution} \times \text{Number of Units} = \text{Total Fixed Costs}$$
$$\text{Number of Units} = \frac{\text{Total Fixed Costs}}{\text{Unit Contribution}}$$

In currency units to reach break-even, one can use the above calculation and multiply by Price, or equivalently use the

$$\text{Break-even(in Sales)} = \frac{\text{Fixed Costs}}{C/P}.$$

Contribution Margin Ratio to compute it as:

R=C Where R is revenue generated C is cost incurred.

a. 1-center problem
b. 120-cell
c. Small numbers game
d. Break-even point

Chapter 1. LINEAR EQUATIONS

11. In mathematics, an _____ is a statement about the relative size or order of two objects, or about whether they are the same or not

- The notation a < b means that a is less than b.
- The notation a > b means that a is greater than b.
- The notation a ≠ b means that a is not equal to b, but does not say that one is bigger than the other or even that they can be compared in size.

In all these cases, a is not equal to b, hence, '_____'.

These relations are known as strict _____

- The notation a ≤ b means that a is less than or equal to b;
- The notation a ≥ b means that a is greater than or equal to b;

An additional use of the notation is to show that one quantity is much greater than another, normally by several orders of magnitude.

- The notation a << b means that a is much less than b.
- The notation a >> b means that a is much greater than b.

If the sense of the _____ is the same for all values of the variables for which its members are defined, then the _____ is called an 'absolute' or 'unconditional' _____. If the sense of an _____ holds only for certain values of the variables involved, but is reversed or destroyed for other values of the variables, it is called a conditional _____.

An _____ may appear unsolvable because it only states whether a number is larger or smaller than another number; but it is possible to apply the same operations for equalities to inequalities. For example, to find x for the _____ 10x > 23 one would divide 23 by 10.

 a. A chemical equation
 b. A posteriori
 c. A Mathematical Theory of Communication
 d. Inequality

12. In mathematics, a _____ is, informally, an infinitely vast and infinitely thin sheet. _____s may be thought of as objects in some higher dimensional space, or they may be considered without any outside space, as in the setting of Euclidean geometry

a. Group
b. Bandwidth
c. Plane
d. Blocking

13. The _____ is one of the coordinates of a point in a two or three-dimensional cartesian coordinate system, equal to the distance of a point from the y-axis in a 2D system, or from the plane of y and z axes in a 3D system, measured along a line parallel to the x axis.
   a. 2-3 heap
   b. 120-cell
   c. X-coordinate
   d. 1-center problem

14. The _____ is the distance between a point and an axis in the Cartesian Coordinate System.
   a. 2-3 heap
   b. 1-center problem
   c. 120-cell
   d. Y-coordinate

15. In differential geometry, a discipline within mathematics, a _____ is a subset of the tangent bundle of a manifold satisfying certain properties. _____s are used to build up notions of integrability, and specifically of a foliation of a manifold
   a. Coherence
   b. Constraint
   c. Discontinuity
   d. Distribution

16. In mathematics, an _____, or central tendency of a data set refers to a measure of the 'middle' or 'expected' value of the data set. There are many different descriptive statistics that can be chosen as a measurement of the central tendency of the data items.

An _____ is a single value that is meant to typify a list of values.

a. A posteriori
b. A chemical equation
c. A Mathematical Theory of Communication
d. Average

17. _____ is used to describe the steepness, incline, gradient, or grade of a straight line. A higher _____ value indicates a steeper incline. The _____ is defined as the ratio of the 'rise' divided by the 'run' between two points on a line, or in other words, the ratio of the altitude change to the horizontal distance between any two points on the line.
   a. Slope
   b. Cognitively Guided Instruction
   c. Point plotting
   d. Number line

18. In mathematics, a _____ is a collection of linear equations involving the same set of variables. For example,

$$\begin{aligned} 3x + 2y - z &= 1 \\ 2x - 2y + 4z &= -2 \\ -x + \tfrac{1}{2}y - z &= 0 \end{aligned}$$

is a system of three equations in the three variables x, y, z. A solution to a linear system is an assignment of numbers to the variables such that all the equations are simultaneously satisfied.

   a. Slutsky equation
   b. Quintic equation
   c. Hypsometric equation
   d. System of linear equations

19. In mathematics, the _____ is an approach to finding a particular solution to certain inhomogeneous ordinary differential equations and recurrence relations. It is closely related to the annihilator method, but instead of using a particular kind of differential operator in order to find the best possible form of the particular solution, a 'guess' is made as to the appropriate form, which is then tested by differentiating the resulting equation. In this sense, the _____ is less formal but more intuitive than the annihilator method.
   a. Linear differential equation
   b. Phase line
   c. Method of undetermined coefficients
   d. Differential algebraic equations

20. _____ is an English dubstep/electronic music duo formed in 2003. The group blends samples, acoustic and electronic instrumentation, and singing from a revolving cast of vocalists. Its members, Adam and Ian, purposefully give very little information about the group or themselves, and tend to do little in the way of self-promotion.

   a. 2-3 heap
   b. Various
   c. 1-center problem
   d. 120-cell

21. The _____ expresses the fact that the difference in the y coordinate between two points on a line that is, $y - y_1$ is proportional to the difference in the x coordinate that is, $x - x_1$. The proportionality constant is m (the slope of the line.

   a. Cobb-Douglas
   b. Rubin Causal Model
   c. Square function
   d. Point-slope form

22. _____ is a form where m is the slope of the line and b is the y-intercept, which is the y-coordinate of the point where the line crosses the y axis. This can be seen by letting $x = 0$, which immediately gives $y = b$.

   a. Slope-intercept form
   b. Dynamical system
   c. Separable extension
   d. Commutative law

23. In mathematics, a _____ is a constant multiplicative factor of a certain object. For example, in the expression $9x^2$, the _____ of x^2 is 9.

The object can be such things as a variable, a vector, a function, etc.

   a. Stability radius
   b. Multivariate division algorithm
   c. Fibonacci polynomials
   d. Coefficient

24. In elementary algebra, a _____ is a polynomial with two terms: the sum of two monomials. It is the simplest kind of polynomial except for a monomial.

The _____ $a^2 - b^2$ can be factored as the product of two other _____s:

$a^2 - b^2$.

The product of a pair of linear _____s $ax + b$ and $cx + d$ is:

$2 + x + bd$.

A _____ raised to the nth power, represented as

n

can be expanded by means of the _____ theorem or, equivalently, using Pascal's triangle.

   a. Rational root theorem
   b. Real structure
   c. Cylindrical algebraic decomposition
   d. Binomial

25. _____ is a geometric term that pertains to the relationship between two vectors. Vectors consist of a 'magnitude' and a 'direction'. Vectors can be said to be _____ when their direction is the same though the magnitude may be different; that is to say, they lie one on top of the other.
   a. Schlegel diagram
   b. Moulton plane
   c. Curve of pursuit
   d. Coincident

26. A _____ of a curve is the envelope of a family of congruent circles centered on the curve. It generalises the concept of _____ lines.

It is sometimes called the offset curve but the term 'offset' often refers also to translation.

   a. Parallel
   b. Cissoid
   c. Bifolium
   d. Cycloid

27. The existence and properties of _____ are the basis of Euclid's parallel postulate. _____ are two lines on the same plane that do not intersect even assuming that lines extend to infinity in either direction.
   a. Spidron
   b. Parallel lines
   c. Vertical translation
   d. Square wheel

28. In mathematics, the _____ of two sets A and B is the set that contains all elements of A that also belong to B, but no other elements.

For explanation of the symbols used in this article, refer to the table of mathematical symbols.

The _____ of A and B

The _____ of A and B is written 'A ∩ B'. Formally:

   x is an element of A ∩ B if and only if
   - x is an element of A and
   - x is an element of B.
   For example:
   - The _____ of the sets {1, 2, 3} and {2, 3, 4} is {2, 3}.
   - The number 9 is not in the _____ of the set of prime numbers {2, 3, 5, 7, 11, â€¦} and the set of odd numbers {1, 3, 5, 7, 9, 11, â€¦}.

If the _____ of two sets A and B is empty, that is they have no elements in common, then they are said to be disjoint, denoted: A ∩ B = Ø. For example the sets {1, 2} and {3, 4} are disjoint, written {1, 2} ∩ {3, 4} = Ø.

   a. Erlang
   b. Order
   c. Advice
   d. Intersection

29. In economics, business, retail, and accounting, a _____ is the value of money that has been used up to produce something, and hence is not available for use anymore. In business, the _____ may be one of acquisition, in which case the amount of money expended to acquire it is counted as _____. In this case, money is the input that is gone in order to acquire the thing.

Chapter 1. LINEAR EQUATIONS

a. 2-3 heap
b. 120-cell
c. 1-center problem
d. Cost

30. A _____ is a set of probability distributions often used for statistical classification. An example of use is the _____ model, which creates a data classification hypothesis from a sum of independent distributions.

- _____ density

a. Generalizability theory
b. Model selection
c. Hidden semi-Markov model
d. Mixture

31. _____s is the social science that studies the production, distribution, and consumption of goods and services.

The term _____s comes from the Ancient Greek οἰκονομῑα (oikonomia, 'management of a household, administration') from οἶκος (oikos, 'house') + νόμος (nomos, 'custom' or 'law'), hence 'rules of the house(hold)'.

Current _____ models developed out of the broader field of political economy in the late 19th century, owing to a desire to use an empirical approach more akin to the physical sciences.

a. Experimental economics
b. A Mathematical Theory of Communication
c. A chemical equation
d. Economic

32. _____ is a fee, paid on borrowed capital. Assets lent include money, shares, consumer goods through hire purchase, major assets such as aircraft, and even entire factories in finance lease arrangements. The _____ is calculated upon the value of the assets in the same manner as upon money.

a. A Mathematical Theory of Communication
b. Interest expense
c. Interest
d. Interest sensitivity gap

Chapter 1. LINEAR EQUATIONS

33. _____ is an economic model describing effects on price and quantity in a market. It predicts that in a competitive market, price will function to equalize the quantity demanded by consumers, and the quantity supplied by producers, resulting in an economic equilibrium of price and quantity. The model incorporates other factors changing equilibrium as a shift of demand and/or supply.
   a. Supply and demand
   b. 1-center problem
   c. Cross price elasticity of demand
   d. Marginal rate of substitution

34. _____ and independent variables refer to values that change in relationship to each other. The _____ are those that are observed to change in response to the independent variables. The independent variables are those that are deliberately manipulated to invoke a change in the _____.
   a. Yates analysis
   b. Steiner system
   c. Dependent variables
   d. Round robin test

35. Dependent variables and _____ refer to values that change in relationship to each other. The dependent variables are those that are observed to change in response to the _____. The _____ are those that are deliberately manipulated to invoke a change in the dependent variables.
   a. One-factor-at-a-time method
   b. Experimental design diagram
   c. Independent variables
   d. Operational confound

36. A _____ is a 2D geometric symbolic representation of information according to some visualization technique. Sometimes, the technique uses a 3D visualization which is then projected onto the 2D surface. The word graph is sometimes used as a synonym for _____.
   a. 2-3 heap
   b. 120-cell
   c. 1-center problem
   d. Diagram

37. In mathematics, the concept of a _____ tries to capture the intuitive idea of a geometrical one-dimensional and continuous object. A simple example is the circle. In everyday use of the term '_____', a straight line is not curved, but in mathematical parlance _____s include straight lines and line segments.

Chapter 1. LINEAR EQUATIONS

  a. Negative pedal curve
  b. Quadrifolium
  c. Kappa curve
  d. Curve

38. _____ is finding a curve which has the best fit to a series of data points and possibly other constraints. This section is an introduction to both interpolation and regression analysis. Both are sometimes used for extrapolation.
  a. Spectral methods
  b. Multiphysics
  c. Numerical stability
  d. Curve fitting

39. In probability theory and statistics, _____ indicates the strength and direction of a linear relationship between two random variables. That is in contrast with the usage of the term in colloquial speech, denoting any relationship, not necessarily linear. In general statistical usage, _____ or co-relation refers to the departure of two random variables from independence.
  a. Sample size
  b. Summary statistics
  c. Random variables
  d. Correlation

40. The _____ is an observable concept in economics that measures the increase in personal consumer spending that occurs with an increase in disposable income. For example, if a household earns one extra dollar of disposable income, and the _____ is 0.65, then of that dollar, the household will spend 65 cents and save 35 cents.

Mathematically, the _____ function is expressed as the derivative of the consumption function with respect to disposable income.

  a. Marginal propensity to consume
  b. 120-cell
  c. 2-3 heap
  d. 1-center problem

41. The _____ refers to the increase in saving that results from an increase in income. For example, if a household earns one extra dollar, and the _____ is 0.35, then of that dollar, the household will spend 65 cents and save 35 cents. It can also go the other way, referring to the decrease in saving that results from a decrease in income.

a. Marginal propensity to save
b. 2-3 heap
c. 1-center problem
d. 120-cell

Chapter 2. SYSTEMS OF LINEAR EQUATIONS; MATRICES

1. In mathematics, a _____ is a rectangular table of elements, which may be numbers or, more generally, any abstract quantities that can be added and multiplied. Matrices are used to describe linear equations, keep track of the coefficients of linear transformations and to record data that depend on multiple parameters. Matrices are described by the field of _____ theory.

    a. Double counting
    b. Coherent
    c. Compression
    d. Matrix

2. In mathematics, a _____ is a collection of linear equations involving the same set of variables. For example,

$$3x + 2y - z = 1$$
$$2x - 2y + 4z = -2$$
$$-x + \tfrac{1}{2}y - z = 0$$

is a system of three equations in the three variables x, y, z. A solution to a linear system is an assignment of numbers to the variables such that all the equations are simultaneously satisfied.

    a. Slutsky equation
    b. System of linear equations
    c. Quintic equation
    d. Hypsometric equation

3. A _____ is an algebraic equation in which each term is either a constant or the product of a constant and a single variable. _____s can have one, two, three or more variables.

    _____s occur with great regularity in applied mathematics.

    a. Quadratic equation
    b. Linear equation
    c. Difference of two squares
    d. Quartic equation

4. In logic, a theory is _____ if it does not contain a contradiction. The lack of contradiction can be defined in either semantic or syntactic terms. The semantic definition states that a theory is _____ if it has a model; this is the sense used in traditional Aristotelian logic, although in contemporary mathematical logic the term satisfiable is used instead.

a. Second-order logic
b. Logic
c. Consistent
d. First-order logic

5. In the study of metric spaces in mathematics, there are various notions of two metrics on the same underlying space being 'the same', or _____.

In the following, M will denote a non-empty set and d_1 and d_2 will denote two metrics on M.

The two metrics d_1 and d_2 are said to be topologically _____ if they generate the same topology on M.

a. A posteriori
b. A chemical equation
c. A Mathematical Theory of Communication
d. Equivalent

6. In linear algebra, the _____ of a matrix is obtained by changing a matrix in some way.

Given the matrices A and B, where:

$$A = \begin{bmatrix} 1 & 3 & 2 \\ 2 & 0 & 1 \\ 5 & 2 & 2 \end{bmatrix}, \quad B = \begin{bmatrix} 4 \\ 3 \\ 1 \end{bmatrix}$$

Then, the _____ is written as:

$$(A|B) = \begin{bmatrix} 1 & 3 & 2 & 4 \\ 2 & 0 & 1 & 3 \\ 5 & 2 & 2 & 1 \end{bmatrix}$$

This is useful when solving systems of linear equations or the _____ may also be used to find the inverse of a matrix by combining it with the identity matrix.

$$C = \begin{bmatrix} 1 & 3 \\ -5 & 0 \end{bmatrix}$$

Let C be a square 2×2 matrix where

To find the inverse of C we create where I is the 2×2 identity matrix.

Chapter 2. SYSTEMS OF LINEAR EQUATIONS; MATRICES

a. Alternating sign matrix
b. Augmented matrix
c. Unimodular polynomial matrix
d. Eigendecomposition

7. In ecology, predation describes a biological interaction where a _____ (an organism that is hunting) feeds on its prey, the organism that is attacked. _____s may or may not kill their prey prior to feeding on them, but the act of predation always results in the death of the prey. The other main category of consumption is detritivory, the consumption of dead organic material (detritus.)
a. Prey
b. 1-center problem
c. Predator
d. 120-cell

8. _____ is a branch of mathematics which focuses on the study of matrices. Initially a sub-branch of linear algebra, it has grown to cover subjects related to graph theory, algebra, combinatorics, and statistics as well.

The term matrix was first coined in 1848 by J.J. Sylvester as a name of an array of numbers.

a. Pairing
b. Segre classification
c. Semi-simple operators
d. Matrix theory

9. In linear algebra a matrix is in _____ if

- All nonzero rows are above any rows of all zeroes, and
- The leading coefficient of a row is always strictly to the right of the leading coefficient of the row above it.

This is the definition used in this article, but some texts add a third condition:

- The leading coefficient of each nonzero row is one.

A matrix is in reduced row echelon form if it satisfies the above three conditions, and if, in addition

- Every leading coefficient is the only nonzero entry in its column.

The first non-zero entry in each row is called a pivot.

This matrix is in reduced row echelon form:

$$\begin{bmatrix} 0 & 1 & 4 & 0 & 0 \\ 0 & 0 & 0 & 1 & 0 \\ 0 & 0 & 0 & 0 & 1 \\ 0 & 0 & 0 & 0 & 0 \end{bmatrix}.$$

The following matrix is also in row echelon form, but not in reduced row form:

$$\begin{bmatrix} 1 & 1 & 1 & 1 \\ 0 & 9 & 0 & 2 \\ 0 & 0 & 0 & 3 \end{bmatrix}.$$

However, this matrix is not in row echelon form, as the leading coefficient of row 3 is not strictly to the right of the leading coefficient of row 2.

$$\begin{bmatrix} 1 & 2 & 3 & 4 \\ 0 & 3 & 7 & 2 \\ 0 & 2 & 0 & 0 \end{bmatrix}$$

Every non-zero matrix can be reduced to an infinite number of echelon forms via elementary matrix transformations.

a. Folded spectrum method
b. Circulant matrix
c. Power iteration
d. Row-echelon form

10. A _____ is a deliberate process for transforming one or more inputs into one or more results, with variable change.

The term is used in a variety of senses, from the very definite arithmetical using an algorithm to the vague heuristics of calculating a strategy in a competition or calculating the chance of a successful relationship between two people.

Multiplying 7 by 8 is a simple algorithmic _____.

Chapter 2. SYSTEMS OF LINEAR EQUATIONS; MATRICES

a. Mathematical maturity
b. Mathematics Subject Classification
c. Mathematical object
d. Calculation

11. In statistics, and particularly in econometrics, the _____ of a system of equations is the result of solving the system for the endogenous variables. This gives the latter as a function of the exogenous variables, if any.

Let Y and X be random vectors.

a. Dynamic factor
b. Log-linear
c. Reduced form
d. Test for structural change

12. In linear algebra, a column vector or _____ is an m × 1 matrix, i.e. a matrix consisting of a single column of m elements.

$$\mathbf{x} = \begin{bmatrix} x_1 \\ x_2 \\ \vdots \\ x_m \end{bmatrix}$$

The transpose of a column vector is a row vector and vice versa.

The set of all column vectors forms a vector space which is the dual space to the set of all row vectors.

a. Spread of a matrix
b. Column Matrix
c. Split-complex number
d. Cayley-Hamilton theorem

13. In linear algebra, a row vector or _____ is a 1 × n matrix, that is, a matrix consisting of a single row:

$$\mathbf{x} = \begin{bmatrix} x_1 & x_2 & \ldots & x_m \end{bmatrix}.$$

The transpose of a row vector is a column vector:

$$\begin{bmatrix} x_1 \\ x_2 \\ \vdots \\ x_m \end{bmatrix} = \begin{bmatrix} x_1 & x_2 & \ldots & x_m \end{bmatrix}^T.$$

The set of all row vectors forms a vector space which is the dual space to the set of all column vectors.

Row vectors are sometimes written using the following non-standard notation:

$$\mathbf{x} = \begin{bmatrix} x_1, x_2, \ldots, x_m \end{bmatrix}.$$

- Matrix multiplication involves the action of multiplying each row vector of one matrix by each column vector of another matrix.

- The dot product of two vectors a and b is equivalent to multiplying the row vector representation of a by the column vector representation of b:

$$\mathbf{a} \cdot \mathbf{b} = \begin{bmatrix} a_1 & a_2 & a_3 \end{bmatrix} \begin{bmatrix} b_1 \\ b_2 \\ b_3 \end{bmatrix}.$$

a. Woodbury matrix identity
b. Row Matrix
c. Gram-Schmidt process
d. Dual vector space

14. In mathematics, _____ is a property that a binary operation can have. It means that, within an expression containing two or more of the same associative operators in a row, the order that the operations are performed does not matter as long as the sequence of the operands is not changed. That is, rearranging the parentheses in such an expression will not change its value.

a. Unital
b. Algebraically closed
c. Idempotence
d. Associativity

15. The _____ is a rule which states that when you add or multiply numbers, changing the order doesn't change the result.
a. Semigroupoid
b. Coimage
c. Conditional event algebra
d. Commutative law

16. In mathematics, the _____ of a number n is the number that, when added to n, yields zero. The _____ of n is denoted −n. For example, 7 is −7, because 7 + (−7) = 0, and the _____ of −0.3 is 0.3, because −0.3 + 0.3 = 0.
a. Additive inverse
b. Algebraic structure
c. Arity
d. Associativity

17. In mathematics, _____ is one of the basic operations defining a vector space in linear algebra. Note that _____ is different from scalar product which is an inner product between two vectors.

More specifically, if K is a field and V is a vector space over K, then _____ is a function from K × V to V.

a. Jordan normal form
b. Scalar multiplication
c. Frobenius normal form
d. Non-negative matrix factorization

18. _____ is the mathematical operation of scaling one number by another. It is one of the four basic operations in elementary arithmetic.

_____ is defined for whole numbers in terms of repeated addition; for example, 4 multiplied by 3 can be calculated by adding 3 copies of 4 together:

$$4 + 4 + 4 = 12.$$

_____ of rational numbers and real numbers is defined by systematic generalization of this basic idea.

a. The number 0 is even.
b. Highest common factor
c. Least common multiple
d. Multiplication

19. In economics, business, retail, and accounting, a _____ is the value of money that has been used up to produce something, and hence is not available for use anymore. In business, the _____ may be one of acquisition, in which case the amount of money expended to acquire it is counted as _____. In this case, money is the input that is gone in order to acquire the thing.
   a. 120-cell
   b. Cost
   c. 1-center problem
   d. 2-3 heap

20. In mathematics, and in particular in abstract algebra, distributivity is a property of binary operations that generalises the _____ law from elementary algebra.
   a. General linear group
   b. Distributive
   c. Closure with a twist
   d. Permutation

21. In mathematics, the term _____ has several different important meanings:

   - An _____ is an equality that remains true regardless of the values of any variables that appear within it, to distinguish it from an equality which is true under more particular conditions. For this, the 'triple bar' symbol ≡ is sometimes used.
   - In algebra, an _____ or _____ element of a set S with a binary operation Â· is an element e that, when combined with any element x of S, produces that same x. That is, eÂ·x = xÂ·e = x for all x in S.
     - The _____ function from a set S to itself, often denoted id or id$_S$, s the function such that i = x for all x in S. This function serves as the _____ element in the set of all functions from S to itself with respect to function composition.
     - In linear algebra, the _____ matrix of size n is the n-by-n square matrix with ones on the main diagonal and zeros elsewhere. This matrix serves as the _____ with respect to matrix multiplication.

A common example of the first meaning is the trigonometric _____

$$\sin^2 \theta + \cos^2 \theta = 1$$

Chapter 2. SYSTEMS OF LINEAR EQUATIONS; MATRICES

which is true for all real values of θ, as opposed to

$$\cos\theta = 1,$$

which is true only for some values of θ, not all. For example, the latter equation is true when $\theta = 0$, false when $\theta = 2$

The concepts of 'additive _____' and 'multiplicative _____' are central to the Peano axioms. The number 0 is the 'additive _____' for integers, real numbers, and complex numbers. For the real numbers, for all $a \in \mathbb{R}$,

$$0 + a = a,$$

$$a + 0 = a, \text{ and}$$

$$0 + 0 = 0.$$

Similarly, The number 1 is the 'multiplicative _____' for integers, real numbers, and complex numbers.

a. Intersection
b. Action
c. Identity
d. ARIA

22. In linear algebra, the _____ or unit matrix of size n is the n-by-n square matrix with ones on the main diagonal and zeros elsewhere. It is denoted by I_n, or simply by I if the size is immaterial or can be trivially determined by the context. (In some fields, such as quantum mechanics, the _____ is denoted by a boldface one, 1; otherwise it is identical to I.)

a. Unital
b. Arity
c. Associativity
d. Identity matrix

23. In algebra, a _____ is a function depending on n that associates a scalar, de, to every n×n square matrix A. The fundamental geometric meaning of a _____ is as the scale factor for measure when A is regarded as a linear transformation. _____s are important both in calculus, where they enter the substitution rule for several variables, and in multilinear algebra.

Chapter 2. SYSTEMS OF LINEAR EQUATIONS; MATRICES

a. Functional determinant
b. 1-center problem
c. Pfaffian
d. Determinant

24. In physics and in _____ calculus, a _____ is a concept characterized by a magnitude and a direction. A _____ can be thought of as an arrow in Euclidean space, drawn from an initial point A pointing to a terminal point B.
   a. Deviation
   b. Dominance
   c. Constraint
   d. Vector

25. _____ is the practice and study of hiding information. In modern times, _____ is considered a branch of both mathematics and computer science, and is affiliated closely with information theory, computer security, and engineering. _____ is used in applications present in technologically advanced societies; examples include the security of ATM cards, computer passwords, and electronic commerce, which all depend on _____.
   a. LOKI
   b. CIKS-1
   c. MAGENTA
   d. Cryptography

26. A _____ is a software program that facilitates symbolic mathematics. The core functionality of a CAS is manipulation of mathematical expressions in symbolic form.

Chapter 2. SYSTEMS OF LINEAR EQUATIONS; MATRICES 25

The symbolic manipulations supported typically include

- simplification to the smallest possible expression or some standard form, including automatic simplification with assumptions and simplification with constraints
- substitution of symbolic, functors or numeric values for expressions
- change of form of expressions: expanding products and powers, partial and full factorization, rewriting as partial fractions, constraint satisfaction, rewriting trigonometric functions as exponentials, etc.
- partial and total differentiation
- symbolic constrained and unconstrained global optimization
- solution of linear and some non-linear equations over various domains
- solution of some differential and difference equations
- taking some limits
- some indefinite and definite integration, including multidimensional integrals
- integral transforms
- arbitrary-precision numeric operations
- Series operations such as expansion, summation and products
- matrix operations including products, inverses, etc.
- display of mathematical expressions in two-dimensional mathematical form, often using typesetting systems similar to TeX
- add-ons for use in applied mathematics such as physics packages for physical computation
- plotting graphs and parametric plots of functions in two and three dimensions, and animating them
- APIs for linking it on an external program such as a database, or using in a programming language to use the _____
- drawing charts and diagrams
- string manipulation such as matching and searching
- statistical computation
- Theorem proving and verification
- graphic production and editing such as CGI and signal processing as image processing
- sound synthesis

Many also include a programming language, allowing users to implement their own algorithms.

Some _____ s focus on a specific area of application; these are typically developed in academia and are free.

a. 2-3 heap
b. 1-center problem
c. Computer algebra system
d. 120-cell

27. The method of _____ or ordinary _____ is used to solve overdetermined systems. _____ is often applied in statistical contexts, particularly regression analysis.

_____ can be interpreted as a method of fitting data.

a. Least squares
b. Non-linear least squares
c. Rata Die
d. System equivalence

28. In linear algebra, the _____ of a matrix A is another matrix A^T created by any one of the following equivalent actions:

- write the rows of A as the columns of A^T
- write the columns of A as the rows of A^T
- reflect A by its main diagonal to obtain A^T

Formally, the _____ of an m × n matrix A is the n × m matrix

$$A^T_{ij} = A_{ji} \text{ for } 1 \leq i \leq n, 1 \leq j \leq m.$$

- $\begin{bmatrix} 1 & 2 \\ 3 & 4 \end{bmatrix}^T = \begin{bmatrix} 1 & 3 \\ 2 & 4 \end{bmatrix}.$

- $\begin{bmatrix} 1 & 2 \\ 3 & 4 \\ 5 & 6 \end{bmatrix}^T = \begin{bmatrix} 1 & 3 & 5 \\ 2 & 4 & 6 \end{bmatrix}.$

For matrices A, B and scalar c we have the following properties of _____:

1. $\left(A^T\right)^T = A$

   Taking the _____ is an involution.

- $(A + B)^T = A^T + B^T$

   The _____ respects addition.

- $(AB)^T = B^T A^T$

Chapter 2. SYSTEMS OF LINEAR EQUATIONS; MATRICES

Note that the order of the factors reverses. From this one can deduce that a square matrix A is invertible if and only if A^T is invertible, and in this case we have $^T = ^{-1}$. It is relatively easy to extend this result to the general case of multiple matrices, where we find that $^T = Z^T Y^T X^T ... C^T B^T A^T$.

- $(c\mathbf{A})^T = c\mathbf{A}^T$

    The _____ of a scalar is the same scalar. Together with, this states that the _____ is a linear map from the space of m × n matrices to the space of all n × m matrices.

- $\det(\mathbf{A}^T) = \det(\mathbf{A})$

    The determinant of a matrix is the same as that of its _____.

- The dot product of two column vectors a and b can be computed as

    $$\mathbf{a} \cdot \mathbf{b} = \mathbf{a}^T \mathbf{b},$$

which is written as $a_i\, b^i$ in Einstein notation.

- If A has only real entries, then $A^T A$ is a positive-semidefinite matrix.
- $(\mathbf{A}^T)^{-1} = (\mathbf{A}^{-1})^T$

    The _____ of an invertible matrix is also invertible, and its inverse is the _____ of the inverse of the original matrix.

- If A is a square matrix, then its eigenvalues are equal to the eigenvalues of its _____.

A square matrix whose _____ is equal to itself is called a symmetric matrix; that is, A is symmetric if

$$\mathbf{A}^T = \mathbf{A}.$$

A square matrix whose _____ is also its inverse is called an orthogonal matrix; that is, G is orthogonal if

$$\mathbf{G}\mathbf{G}^T = \mathbf{G}^T\mathbf{G} = \mathbf{I}_n,$$ the identity matrix.

A square matrix whose _____ is equal to its negative is called skew-symmetric matrix; that is, A is skew-symmetric if

$$\mathbf{A}^T = -\mathbf{A}.$$

The conjugate _____ of the complex matrix A, written as A*, is obtained by taking the _____ of A and the complex conjugate of each entry:

$$\mathbf{A}^* = (\overline{\mathbf{A}})^{\mathrm{T}} = \overline{(\mathbf{A}^{\mathrm{T}})}.$$

If f: V→W is a linear map between vector spaces V and W with nondegenerate bilinear forms, we define the _____ of f to be the linear map $^t f$: W→V, determined by

$$B_V(v,\,^t f(w)) = B_W(f(v), w) \quad \forall\, v \in V, w \in W.$$

Here, B_V and B_W are the bilinear forms on V and W respectively. The matrix of the _____ of a map is the transposed matrix only if the bases are orthonormal with respect to their bilinear forms.

Over a complex vector space, one often works with sesquilinear forms instead of bilinear.

a. Cartan matrix
b. Tridiagonal matrix
c. Polynomial matrix
d. Transpose

Chapter 3. LINEAR PROGRAMMING: GEOMETRIC APPROACH

1. In mathematics, an _____ is a statement about the relative size or order of two objects, or about whether they are the same or not

- The notation a < b means that a is less than b.
- The notation a > b means that a is greater than b.
- The notation a ≠ b means that a is not equal to b, but does not say that one is bigger than the other or even that they can be compared in size.

In all these cases, a is not equal to b, hence, '_____'.

These relations are known as strict _____

- The notation a ≤ b means that a is less than or equal to b;
- The notation a ≥ b means that a is greater than or equal to b;

An additional use of the notation is to show that one quantity is much greater than another, normally by several orders of magnitude.

- The notation a << b means that a is much less than b.
- The notation a >> b means that a is much greater than b.

If the sense of the _____ is the same for all values of the variables for which its members are defined, then the _____ is called an 'absolute' or 'unconditional' _____. If the sense of an _____ holds only for certain values of the variables involved, but is reversed or destroyed for other values of the variables, it is called a conditional _____.

An _____ may appear unsolvable because it only states whether a number is larger or smaller than another number; but it is possible to apply the same operations for equalities to inequalities. For example, to find x for the _____ 10x > 23 one would divide 23 by 10.

a. Inequality
b. A Mathematical Theory of Communication
c. A posteriori
d. A chemical equation

2. A set S of real numbers is called _____ from above if there is a real number k such that k ≥ s for all s in S. The number k is called an upper bound of S. The terms _____ from below and lower bound are similarly defined.
a. Descent
b. Derivative algebra
c. Harmonic series
d. Bounded

Chapter 3. LINEAR PROGRAMMING: GEOMETRIC APPROACH

3. A _____ is a set of probability distributions often used for statistical classification. An example of use is the _____ model, which creates a data classification hypothesis from a sum of independent distributions.

- _____ density

a. Hidden semi-Markov model
b. Generalizability theory
c. Model selection
d. Mixture

4. In mathematics, a _____ is a condition that a solution to an optimization problem must satisfy. There are two types of _____s: equality _____s and inequality _____s. The set of solutions that satisfy all _____s is called the feasible set.

a. Foci
b. Decidable
c. Concurrent
d. Constraint

5. In mathematics, _____ is a technique for optimization of a linear objective function, subject to linear equality and linear inequality constraints. Informally, _____ determines the way to achieve the best outcome in a given mathematical model given some list of requirements represented as linear equations.

More formally, given a polytope, and a real-valued affine function

$$f(x_1, x_2, \ldots, x_n) = c_1 x_1 + c_2 x_2 + \cdots + c_n x_n + d$$

defined on this polytope, a _____ method will find a point in the polytope where this function has the smallest value.

a. Descent direction
b. Linear programming
c. Lin-Kernighan
d. Linear programming relaxation

6. An _____ is a tree data structure in which each internal node has up to eight children. _____s are most often used to partition a three dimensional space by recursively subdividing it into eight octants. _____s are the three-dimensional analog of quadtrees.

a. External node
b. Octree
c. Interval tree
d. Adaptive k-d tree

7. The mathematical concept of a _____ expresses the intuitive idea of deterministic dependence between two quantities, one of which is viewed as primary and the other as secondary. A _____ then is a way to associate a unique output for each input of a specified type, for example, a real number or an element of a given set.

a. Going up
b. Coherent
c. Grill
d. Function

8. In mathematics, a _____ is a statement that can be proved on the basis of explicitly stated or previously agreed assumptions.

a. Logical value
b. Disjunction introduction
c. Boolean function
d. Theorem

9. _____ is an economics theory, that refers to individuals or societies gaining the maximum amount out of the resources they have available to them. The theory proposed by most economists is that _____ refers to the _____ of profit.

As some economists have begun to find out, this theory does not hold true for all people and cultures.

a. Homogeneity
b. Boundary
c. Composite
d. Maximization

Chapter 4. LINEAR PROGRAMMING: SIMPLEX METHOD

1. In geometry, a _____ or n-_____ is an n-dimensional analogue of a triangle. Specifically, a _____ is the convex hull of a set of affinely independent points in some Euclidean space of dimension n or higher.

For example, a 0-_____ is a point, a 1-_____ is a line segment, a 2-_____ is a triangle, a 3-_____ is a tetrahedron, and a 4-_____ is a pentachoron.

a. Demihypercubes
b. Hypercell
c. Polytetrahedron
d. Simplex

2. In mathematical optimization theory, the simplex algorithm, created by the American mathematician George Dantzig in 1947, is a popular algorithm for numerical solution of the linear programming problem. The journal Computing in Science and Engineering listed it as one of the top 10 algorithms of the century.

An unrelated, but similarly named method is the Nelder-Mead method or downhill _____ due to Nelder ' Mead and is a numerical method for optimising many-dimensional unconstrained problems, belonging to the more general class of search algorithms.

a. Differential evolution
b. Fibonacci search
c. Hill climbing
d. Simplex method

3. In mathematics, _____ is a technique for optimization of a linear objective function, subject to linear equality and linear inequality constraints. Informally, _____ determines the way to achieve the best outcome in a given mathematical model given some list of requirements represented as linear equations.

More formally, given a polytope, and a real-valued affine function

$$f(x_1, x_2, \ldots, x_n) = c_1 x_1 + c_2 x_2 + \cdots + c_n x_n + d$$

defined on this polytope, a _____ method will find a point in the polytope where this function has the smallest value.

a. Descent direction
b. Linear programming
c. Lin-Kernighan
d. Linear programming relaxation

Chapter 4. LINEAR PROGRAMMING: SIMPLEX METHOD

4. _____, also sometimes known as standard form or as exponential notation, is a way of writing numbers that accommodates values too large or small to be conveniently written in standard decimal notation. _____ has a number of useful properties and is often favored by scientists, mathematicians and engineers, who work with such numbers.

In _____, numbers are written in the form:

$$a \times 10^b$$

a. Scientific notation
b. Radix point
c. 1-center problem
d. Leading zero

5. In Linear programming a _____ is a variable which is added to a constraint to turn the inequality into an equation. This is required to turn an inequality into an equality where a linear combination of variables is less than or equal to a given constant in the former. As with the other variables in the augmented constraints, the _____ cannot take on negative values, as the Simplex algorithm requires them to be positive or zero.

a. Bellman equation
b. Slack variable
c. Shape optimization
d. Shekel function

6. In mathematics, a _____ is a rectangular table of elements, which may be numbers or, more generally, any abstract quantities that can be added and multiplied. Matrices are used to describe linear equations, keep track of the coefficients of linear transformations and to record data that depend on multiple parameters. Matrices are described by the field of _____ theory.

a. Matrix
b. Double counting
c. Compression
d. Coherent

7. Initial objects are also called _____, and terminal objects are also called final.

a. Coterminal
b. Direct limit
c. Terminal object
d. Colimit

8. In mathematical optimization theory, the _____, created by the North American mathematician George Dantzig in 1947, is a popular technique for numerical solution of the linear programming problem.

   a. Simplex algorithm
   b. Feit–Thompson theorem
   c. Partition
   d. Sociable number

9. In ecology, predation describes a biological interaction where a _____ (an organism that is hunting) feeds on its prey, the organism that is attacked. _____s may or may not kill their prey prior to feeding on them, but the act of predation always results in the death of the prey. The other main category of consumption is detritivory, the consumption of dead organic material (detritus.)

   a. Prey
   b. Predator
   c. 120-cell
   d. 1-center problem

10. In mathematics, an _____ or member of a set is any one of the distinct objects that make up that set.

Writing A = {1,2,3,4}, means that the _____s of the set A are the numbers 1, 2, 3 and 4. Groups of _____s of A, for example {1,2}, are subsets of A.

   a. Order
   b. Ideal
   c. Universal code
   d. Element

11. _____ is an economics theory, that refers to individuals or societies gaining the maximum amount out of the resources they have available to them. The theory proposed by most economists is that _____ refers to the _____ of profit.

As some economists have begun to find out, this theory does not hold true for all people and cultures.

   a. Composite
   b. Homogeneity
   c. Boundary
   d. Maximization

Chapter 4. LINEAR PROGRAMMING: SIMPLEX METHOD

12. _____ is a part of mathematics concerned with questions of size, shape, and relative position of figures and with properties of space. _____ is one of the oldest sciences. Initially a body of practical knowledge concerning lengths, areas, and volumes, in the third century BC _____ was put into an axiomatic form by Euclid, whose treatment--Euclidean _____--set a standard for many centuries to follow.
  a. Geometry
  b. 1-center problem
  c. 2-3 heap
  d. 120-cell

13. In the mathematical area of order theory, every partially ordered set P gives rise to a _____ partially ordered set which is often denoted by P^{op} or P^d. This _____ order P^{op} is defined to be the set with the inverse order. It is easy to see that this construction, which can be depicted by flipping the Hasse diagram for P upside down, will indeed yield a partially ordered set.
  a. Context-sensitive language
  b. Contraction mapping
  c. Christofides heuristics
  d. Dual

14. In linear programming, the primary problem and the _____ are complementary. A solution to either one determines a solution to both.

Linear programming problems are optimization problems in which the objective function and the constraints are all linear.

  a. Topological derivative
  b. Linear programming relaxation
  c. Linear matrix inequality
  d. Dual problem

15. In the geometry of the projective plane, _____ refers to geometric transformations that replace points by lines and lines by points while preserving incidence properties among the transformed objects. The existence of such transformations leads to a general principle, that any theorem about incidences between points and lines in the projective plane may be transformed into another theorem about lines and points, by a substitution of the appropriate words.

_____ in the projective plane is a special case of _____ for projective spaces, transformations that interchange

   dimension + codimension.

a. Decidable
b. Duality
c. Disk
d. Blocking

16. In linear algebra, the _____ of a matrix A is another matrix A^T created by any one of the following equivalent actions:

- write the rows of A as the columns of A^T
- write the columns of A as the rows of A^T
- reflect A by its main diagonal to obtain A^T

Formally, the _____ of an m × n matrix A is the n × m matrix

$$A^T_{ij} = A_{ji} \text{ for } 1 \leq i \leq n, 1 \leq j \leq m.$$

- $\begin{bmatrix} 1 & 2 \\ 3 & 4 \end{bmatrix}^T = \begin{bmatrix} 1 & 3 \\ 2 & 4 \end{bmatrix}.$

- $\begin{bmatrix} 1 & 2 \\ 3 & 4 \\ 5 & 6 \end{bmatrix}^T = \begin{bmatrix} 1 & 3 & 5 \\ 2 & 4 & 6 \end{bmatrix}.$

For matrices A, B and scalar c we have the following properties of _____:

1. $\left(A^T\right)^T = A$

   Taking the _____ is an involution.

- $(A + B)^T = A^T + B^T$

   The _____ respects addition.

- $(AB)^T = B^T A^T$

Chapter 4. LINEAR PROGRAMMING: SIMPLEX METHOD

Note that the order of the factors reverses. From this one can deduce that a square matrix A is invertible if and only if A^T is invertible, and in this case we have $^T = ^{-1}$. It is relatively easy to extend this result to the general case of multiple matrices, where we find that^T = $Z^T Y^T X^T ... C^T B^T A^T$.

- $(c\mathbf{A})^T = c\mathbf{A}^T$

  The _____ of a scalar is the same scalar. Together with, this states that the _____ is a linear map from the space of m × n matrices to the space of all n × m matrices.

- $\det(\mathbf{A}^T) = \det(\mathbf{A})$

  The determinant of a matrix is the same as that of its _____.

- The dot product of two column vectors a and b can be computed as

  $$\mathbf{a} \cdot \mathbf{b} = \mathbf{a}^T \mathbf{b},$$

which is written as $a_i b^i$ in Einstein notation.
- If A has only real entries, then $A^T A$ is a positive-semidefinite matrix.
- $(\mathbf{A}^T)^{-1} = (\mathbf{A}^{-1})^T$

  The _____ of an invertible matrix is also invertible, and its inverse is the _____ of the inverse of the original matrix.

- If A is a square matrix, then its eigenvalues are equal to the eigenvalues of its _____.

A square matrix whose _____ is equal to itself is called a symmetric matrix; that is, A is symmetric if

$$\mathbf{A}^T = \mathbf{A}.$$

A square matrix whose _____ is also its inverse is called an orthogonal matrix; that is, G is orthogonal if

$$\mathbf{G}\mathbf{G}^T = \mathbf{G}^T\mathbf{G} = \mathbf{I}_n,$$ the identity matrix.

A square matrix whose _____ is equal to its negative is called skew-symmetric matrix; that is, A is skew-symmetric if

$$\mathbf{A}^T = -\mathbf{A}.$$

The conjugate _____ of the complex matrix A, written as A*, is obtained by taking the _____ of A and the complex conjugate of each entry:

$$\mathbf{A}^* = (\overline{\mathbf{A}})^{\mathrm{T}} = \overline{(\mathbf{A}^{\mathrm{T}})}.$$

If f: V→W is a linear map between vector spaces V and W with nondegenerate bilinear forms, we define the _____ of f to be the linear map ᵗf : W→V, determined by

$$B_V(v, {}^t f(w)) = B_W(f(v), w) \quad \forall\, v \in V, w \in W.$$

Here, B_V and B_W are the bilinear forms on V and W respectively. The matrix of the _____ of a map is the transposed matrix only if the bases are orthonormal with respect to their bilinear forms.

Over a complex vector space, one often works with sesquilinear forms instead of bilinear.

a. Cartan matrix
b. Tridiagonal matrix
c. Polynomial matrix
d. Transpose

17. In mathematics, a _____ is a condition that a solution to an optimization problem must satisfy. There are two types of _____s: equality _____s and inequality _____s. The set of solutions that satisfy all _____s is called the feasible set.
a. Constraint
b. Decidable
c. Concurrent
d. Foci

18. In game theory, a player's _____ in a game is a complete plan of action for whatever situation might arise; this fully determines the player's behaviour. A player's _____ will determine the action the player will take at any stage of the game, for every possible history of play up to that stage.

A _____ profile is a set of strategies for each player which fully specifies all actions in a game.

a. Sir Philip Sidney game
b. Strategy
c. Matching pennies
d. Correlated equilibrium

Chapter 5. FINANCE

1. _____ is a fee, paid on borrowed capital. Assets lent include money, shares, consumer goods through hire purchase, major assets such as aircraft, and even entire factories in finance lease arrangements. The _____ is calculated upon the value of the assets in the same manner as upon money.

   a. A Mathematical Theory of Communication
   b. Interest expense
   c. Interest sensitivity gap
   d. Interest

2. In abstract algebra, a module S over a ring R is called _____ or irreducible if it is not the zero module 0 and if its only submodules are 0 and S. Understanding the _____ modules over a ring is usually helpful because these modules form the 'building blocks' of all other modules in a certain sense.

   Abelian groups are the same as Z-modules.

   a. Derivation
   b. Harmonic series
   c. Basis
   d. Simple

3. _____ is a general term for any type of information processing. This includes phenomena ranging from human thinking to calculations with a more narrow meaning. _____ is a process following a well-defined model that is understood and can be expressed in an algorithm, protocol, network topology, etc.

   a. 2-3 heap
   b. 120-cell
   c. 1-center problem
   d. Computation

4. _____ is the concept of adding accumulated interest back to the principal, so that interest is earned on interest from that moment on. The act of declaring interest to be principal is called compounding. A loan, for example, may have its interest compounded every month: in this case, a loan with $100 principal and 1% interest per month would have a balance of $101 at the end of the first month.

   a. Retained interest
   b. Compound interest
   c. Net interest margin
   d. Net interest margin securities

Chapter 5. FINANCE

5. In mathematics, a _____ is a number that can be expressed as an integral of an algebraic function over an algebraic domain. Kontsevich and Zagier define a _____ as a complex number whose real and imaginary parts are values of absolutely convergent integrals of rational functions with rational coefficients, over domains in given by polynomial inequalities with rational coefficients.

   a. Disk
   b. Boussinesq approximation
   c. Closeness
   d. Period

6. _____ or amortisation is the process of decreasing an amount over a period of time. The word comes from Middle English amortisen to kill, alienate in mortmain, from Anglo-French amorteser, alteration of amortir, from Vulgar Latin admortire to kill, from Latin ad- + mort-, mors death. Particular instances of the term include:

   - _____, the allocation of a lump sum amount to different time periods, particularly for loans and other forms of finance, including related interest or other finance charges.
     - _____ schedule, a table detailing each periodic payment on a loan, as generated by an _____ calculator.
     - Negative _____, an _____ schedule where the loan amount actually increases through not paying the full interest
   - Amortized analysis, analyzing the execution cost of algorithms over a sequence of operations.
   - _____ of capital expenditures of certain assets under accounting rules, particularly intangible assets, in a manner analogous to depreciation.
   - _____

_____ is also used in the context of zoning regulations and describes the time in which a property owner has to relocate when the property's use constitutes a preexisting nonconforming use under zoning regulations.

   - Depreciation

   a. Identity
   b. Amortization
   c. ISAAC
   d. Origin

7. A _____ is the transfer of an interest in property (or in law the equivalent - a charge) to a lender as a security for a debt - usually a loan of money. While a _____ in itself is not a debt, it is lender's security for a debt. It is a transfer of an interest in land (or the equivalent), from the owner to the _____ lender, on the condition that this interest will be returned to the owner of the real estate when the terms of the _____ have been satisfied or performed.

Chapter 5. FINANCE

   a. 2-3 heap
   b. Mortgage
   c. 120-cell
   d. 1-center problem

8. In mathematics and in the sciences, a _____ (plural: _____e, formulæ or _____s) is a concise way of expressing information symbolically (as in a mathematical or chemical _____), or a general relationship between quantities. One of many famous _____e is Albert Einstein's E = mc² (see special relativity

In mathematics, a _____ is a key to solve an equation with variables. For example, the problem of determining the volume of a sphere is one that requires a significant amount of integral calculus to solve.

   a. 1-center problem
   b. 2-3 heap
   c. 120-cell
   d. Formula

9. The term _____ refers to the central sense organ complex, for those animals that have one, normally on the ventral surface of the head and can depending on the definition in the human case, include the hair, forehead, eyebrow, eyes, nose, ears, cheeks, mouth, lips, philtrum, teeth, skin, and chin. The _____ has uses of expression, appearance, and identity amongst others.It also has different senses like smelling, tasting, hearing, and seeing.

Caricatures often exaggerate facial features to make a _____ more easily recognized in association with a pronounced portion of the _____ of the individual in question--for example, a caricature of Osama bin Laden might focus on his facial hair and nose; a caricature of George W. Bush might enlarge his ears to the size of an elephant¢s; a caricature of Jay Leno may pronounce his head and chin; and a caricature of Mick Jagger might enlarge his lips.

   a. 120-cell
   b. 1-center problem
   c. Face
   d. 2-3 heap

Chapter 6. SETS; COUNTING TECHNIQUES

1. In mathematics, the _____ is a term used to describe the number of times one must apply a given operation to an integer before reaching a fixed point.

Usually, this refers to the additive or multiplicative persistence of an integer, which is how often one has to replace the number by the sum or product of its digits until one reaches a single digit. Because the numbers are broken down into their digits, the additive or multiplicative persistence depends on the radix.

   a. Lychrel number
   b. Coprime
   c. Linear congruence theorem
   d. Persistence of a number

2. In mathematics, an _____ or member of a set is any one of the distinct objects that make up that set.

Writing A = {1,2,3,4}, means that the _____s of the set A are the numbers 1, 2, 3 and 4. Groups of _____s of A, for example {1,2}, are subsets of A.

   a. Element
   b. Order
   c. Ideal
   d. Universal code

3. In mathematics, and more specifically set theory, the _____ is the unique set having no members. Some axiomatic set theories assure that the _____ exists by including an axiom of _____; in other theories, its existence can be deduced. Many possible properties of sets are trivially true for the _____.

   a. A Mathematical Theory of Communication
   b. Empty function
   c. Inverse function
   d. Empty set

4. In mathematics, a _____ is a set that is negligible in some sense. For different applications, the meaning of 'negligible' varies. In measure theory, any set of measure 0 is called a _____.

   a. Borel-Cantelli lemma
   b. Prevalence and shyness
   c. Radonifying function
   d. Null set

5. In mathematics, especially in set theory, a set A is a _____ of a set B if A is 'contained' inside B. Notice that A and B may coincide. The relationship of one set being a _____ of another is called inclusion.

Chapter 6. SETS; COUNTING TECHNIQUES

   a. Set of all sets
   b. Cartesian product
   c. Horizontal line test
   d. Subset

6. _____ is a branch of mathematics which focuses on the study of matrices. Initially a sub-branch of linear algebra, it has grown to cover subjects related to graph theory, algebra, combinatorics, and statistics as well.

The term matrix was first coined in 1848 by J.J. Sylvester as a name of an array of numbers.

   a. Pairing
   b. Segre classification
   c. Semi-simple operators
   d. Matrix theory

7. In set theory, the term _____ refers to a set operation used in the convergence of set elements to form a resultant set containing the elements of both sets. As a simple example, a _____ of two disjoint sets, which do not have elements in common results in a set containing all elements from both sets. A Venn diagram representing the _____ of sets A and B.
   a. Union
   b. UES
   c. Event
   d. Introduction

8. _____ or set diagrams are diagrams that show all hypothetically possible logical relations between a finite collection of sets. _____ were invented around 1880 by John Venn. They are used in many fields, including set theory, probability, logic, statistics, and computer science.
   a. 2-3 heap
   b. Venn diagrams
   c. 1-center problem
   d. 120-cell

9. A _____ is a 2D geometric symbolic representation of information according to some visualization technique. Sometimes, the technique uses a 3D visualization which is then projected onto the 2D surface. The word graph is sometimes used as a synonym for _____.

a. 1-center problem
b. Diagram
c. 2-3 heap
d. 120-cell

10. In mathematics, the _____ of two sets A and B is the set that contains all elements of A that also belong to B, but no other elements.

For explanation of the symbols used in this article, refer to the table of mathematical symbols.

The _____ of A and B

The _____ of A and B is written 'A ∩ B'. Formally:

   x is an element of A ∩ B if and only if
   - x is an element of A and
   - x is an element of B.
   For example:
   - The _____ of the sets {1, 2, 3} and {2, 3, 4} is {2, 3}.
   - The number 9 is not in the _____ of the set of prime numbers {2, 3, 5, 7, 11, …} and the set of odd numbers {1, 3, 5, 7, 9, 11, …}.

If the _____ of two sets A and B is empty, that is they have no elements in common, then they are said to be disjoint, denoted: A ∩ B = Ø. For example the sets {1, 2} and {3, 4} are disjoint, written
{1, 2} ∩ {3, 4} = Ø.

a. Erlang
b. Advice
c. Order
d. Intersection

11. In mathematics, the _____ is an approach to finding a particular solution to certain inhomogeneous ordinary differential equations and recurrence relations. It is closely related to the annihilator method, but instead of using a particular kind of differential operator in order to find the best possible form of the particular solution, a 'guess' is made as to the appropriate form, which is then tested by differentiating the resulting equation. In this sense, the _____ is less formal but more intuitive than the annihilator method.

a. Linear differential equation
b. Phase line
c. Differential algebraic equations
d. Method of undetermined coefficients

12. In discrete mathematics and predominantly in set theory, a _____ is a concept used in comparisons of sets to refer to the unique values of one set in relation to another. The terms 'absolute' and 'relative' _____ refer to more specific applications of the concept, with universal _____s referring to elements unique to the universal set and the latter referring to the unique elements of one set in relation to another. In this Image, the universal set is represented by the border of the image, and the set A as a disc.
a. Derivative algebra
b. Kernel
c. Huge
d. Complement

13. In mathematics, two sets are said to be disjoint if they have no element in common. For example, {1, 2, 3} and {4, 5, 6} are _____.

Formally, two sets A and B are disjoint if their intersection is the empty set.
wikimedia.org/math/b/3/5/b35d3befc06b831ff4d6cd63bf922efb.png">

This definition extends to any collection of sets.

a. Horizontal line test
b. Preimage
c. Subset
d. Disjoint sets

14. In probability theory, an _____ is a set of outcomes to which a probability is assigned. Typically, when the sample space is finite, any subset of the sample space is an _____. However, this approach does not work well in cases where the sample space is infinite, most notably when the outcome is a real number.
a. Equaliser
b. Information set
c. Audio compression
d. Event

Chapter 6. SETS; COUNTING TECHNIQUES

15. In logic and philosophy, _____ refers to either (a) the 'content' or 'meaning' of a meaningful declarative sentence or (b) the pattern of symbols, marks, or sounds that make up a meaningful declarative sentence. _____s in either case are intended to be truth-bearers, that is, they are either true or false.

The existence of _____s in the former sense, as well as the existence of 'meanings', is disputed.

   a. Proposition
   b. Laws of classical logic
   c. Linear logic
   d. Logicism

16. _____ is the study of mathematical structures that are fundamentally discrete in the sense of not supporting or requiring the notion of continuity. Objects studied in _____ are largely countable sets such as integers, finite graphs, and formal languages.

_____ has become popular in recent decades because of its applications to computer science.

   a. Discrete mathematics
   b. Pooling design
   c. Dual graph
   d. Partial equivalence relation

17. In mathematics and in the sciences, a _____ (plural: _____e, formulæ or _____s) is a concise way of expressing information symbolically (as in a mathematical or chemical _____), or a general relationship between quantities. One of many famous _____e is Albert Einstein's $E = mc^2$ (see special relativity

In mathematics, a _____ is a key to solve an equation with variables. For example, the problem of determining the volume of a sphere is one that requires a significant amount of integral calculus to solve.

   a. Formula
   b. 2-3 heap
   c. 120-cell
   d. 1-center problem

18. _____ is the mathematical operation of scaling one number by another. It is one of the four basic operations in elementary arithmetic.

Chapter 6. SETS; COUNTING TECHNIQUES

_____ is defined for whole numbers in terms of repeated addition; for example, 4 multiplied by 3 can be calculated by adding 3 copies of 4 together:

$$4 + 4 + 4 = 12.$$

_____ of rational numbers and real numbers is defined by systematic generalization of this basic idea.

a. The number 0 is even.
b. Highest common factor
c. Multiplication
d. Least common multiple

19. In set theory, a _____ is a partially ordered set such that for each $t \in T$, the set $\{s \in T : s < t\}$ is well-ordered by the relation <. For each $t \in T$, the order type of $\{s \in T : s < t\}$ is called the height of t. The height of T itself is the least ordinal greater than the height of each element of T.

a. Transitive reduction
b. Definable numbers
c. Set-theoretic topology
d. Tree

20. In several fields of mathematics the term _____ is used with different but closely related meanings. They all relate to the notion of mapping the elements of a set to other elements of the same set, i.e., exchanging elements of a set.

The general concept of _____ can be defined more formally in different contexts:

In combinatorics, a _____ is usually understood to be a sequence containing each element from a finite set once, and only once.

a. Linearly independent
b. Cyclic permutation
c. Tensor product
d. Permutation

21. In mathematics, the _____ of a non-negative integer n, denoted by n!, is the product of all positive integers less than or equal to n. For example,

$$5! = 1 \times 2 \times 3 \times 4 \times 5 = 120$$

and
$$6! = 1 \times 2 \times 3 \times 4 \times 5 \times 6 = 720$$

The notation n! was introduced by Christian Kramp in 1808.

The _____ function is formally defined by

$$n! = \prod_{k=1}^{n} k \qquad \forall n \in \mathbb{N}.$$

The above definition incorporates the instance

$$0! = 1$$

as an instance of the fact that the product of no numbers at all is 1.

- a. Symbolic combinatorics
- b. Factorial
- c. Partition of a set
- d. Plane partition

22. In combinatorial mathematics, a _____ is an un-ordered collection of distinct elements, usually of a prescribed size and taken from a given set. Given such a set S, a _____ of elements of S is just a subset of S, where as always forsets the order of the elements is not taken into account. Also, as always forsets, no elements can be repeated more than once in a _____; this is often referred to as a 'collection without repetition'.

- a. Heawood number
- b. Sparsity
- c. Fill-in
- d. Combination

23. In category theory, an abstract branch of mathematics, an _____ of a category C is an object I in C such that for every object X in C, there exists precisely one morphism I → X. The dual notion is that of a terminal object: T is terminal if for every object X in C there exists a single morphism X → T. _____ s are also called coterminal, and terminal objects are also called final.

a. A posteriori
b. A Mathematical Theory of Communication
c. A chemical equation
d. Initial object

24. In elementary algebra, a _____ is a polynomial with two terms: the sum of two monomials. It is the simplest kind of polynomial except for a monomial.

The _____ $a^2 - b^2$ can be factored as the product of two other _____s:

$a^2 - b^2$.

The product of a pair of linear _____s $ax + b$ and $cx + d$ is:

$2 + x + bd$.

A _____ raised to the nth power, represented as

n

can be expanded by means of the _____ theorem or, equivalently, using Pascal's triangle.

a. Real structure
b. Rational root theorem
c. Binomial
d. Cylindrical algebraic decomposition

25. In mathematics, the _____ $\binom{n}{k}$ is the coefficient of the x^k term in the polynomial expansion of the binomial power n.

In combinatorics, $\binom{n}{k}$ is interpreted as the number of k-element subsets of an n-element set, that is the number of ways that k things can be 'chosen' from a set of n things. Hence, $\binom{n}{k}$ is often read as 'n choose k' and called the choose function of n and k.

Chapter 6. SETS; COUNTING TECHNIQUES

a. Rule of product
b. Dyson conjecture
c. Symbolic combinatorics
d. Binomial coefficient

26. In mathematics, the _____ is an important formula giving the expansion of powers of sums. Its simplest version states that

$$(x+y)^n = \sum_{k=0}^{n} \binom{n}{k} x^{n-k} y^k \quad (1)$$

for any real or complex numbers x and y, and any nonnegative integer n. The binomial coefficient appearing in may be defined in terms of the factorial function n!:

$$\binom{n}{k} = \frac{n!}{k!(n-k)!}.$$

For example, here are the cases where 2 ≤ n ≤ 5:

$$(x+y)^2 = x^2 + 2xy + y^2$$
$$(x+y)^3 = x^3 + 3x^2y + 3xy^2 + y^3$$
$$(x+y)^4 = x^4 + 4x^3y + 6x^2y^2 + 4xy^3 + y^4$$
$$(x+y)^5 = x^5 + 5x^4y + 10x^3y^2 + 10x^2y^3 + 5xy^4 + y^5.$$

Formula is valid more generally for any elements x and y of a semiring as long as xy = yx..

a. Stirling transform
b. Hypergeometric identities
c. Lah numbers
d. Binomial theorem

27. In mathematics, a _____ is a constant multiplicative factor of a certain object. For example, in the expression $9x^2$, the _____ of x^2 is 9.

The object can be such things as a variable, a vector, a function, etc.

a. Coefficient
b. Fibonacci polynomials
c. Stability radius
d. Multivariate division algorithm

28. In mathematics, a _____ is a statement that can be proved on the basis of explicitly stated or previously agreed assumptions.
   a. Boolean function
   b. Disjunction introduction
   c. Logical value
   d. Theorem

29. A _____ is one of the basic shapes of geometry: a polygon with three corners or vertices and three sides or edges which are line segments. A _____ with vertices A, B, and C is denoted ABC.

In Euclidean geometry any three non-collinear points determine a unique _____ and a unique plane.

   a. Kepler triangle
   b. 1-center problem
   c. Triangle
   d. Fuhrmann circle

Chapter 7. PROBABILITY

1. In probability theory, an _____ is a set of outcomes to which a probability is assigned. Typically, when the sample space is finite, any subset of the sample space is an _____. However, this approach does not work well in cases where the sample space is infinite, most notably when the outcome is a real number.

    a. Equaliser
    b. Audio compression
    c. Information set
    d. Event

2. In game theory, an _____ is a set of moves or strategies taken by the players, or their payoffs resulting from the actions or strategies taken by all players. The two are complementary in that given knowledge of the set of strategies of all players, the final state of the game is known, as are any relevant payoffs. In a game where chance or a random event is involved, the _____ is not known from only the set of strategies, but is only realized when the random even are realized.

    a. Autonomous system
    b. Algebraic
    c. Equaliser
    d. Outcome

3. _____ is the likelihood or chance that something is the case or will happen. Theoretical _____ is used extensively in areas such as statistics, mathematics, science and philosophy to draw conclusions about the likelihood of potential events and the underlying mechanics of complex systems.

    The word _____ does not have a consistent direct definition.

    a. Standardized moment
    b. Discrete random variable
    c. Probability
    d. Statistical significance

4. _____ is a notion in statistics and probability theory that random events exhibit regularity when repeated enough times or that enough sufficiently similar random events exhibit regularity. It is an umbrella term that covers the law of large numbers, all central limit theorems and ergodic theorems.

    If one throws a die once, it is difficult to predict the outcome, but if we repeat this experiment many times, we will see that the number of times each result occurs divided by the number of throws will eventually stabilize towards a specific value.

a. Random variate
b. Skewness risk
c. Statistical regularity
d. Statistical assembly

5. In mathematics, a _____, named after Andrey Markov, is a stochastic process with the Markov property. Having the Markov property means that, given the present state, future states are independent of the past states. In other words, the description of the present state fully captures all the information that could influence the future evolution of the process. Future states will be reached through a probabilistic process instead of a deterministic one.
   a. Possibility theory
   b. Law of Truly Large Numbers
   c. Markov chain
   d. Variance-to-mean ratio

6. In statistics, a _____ is a subset of a population. Typically, the population is very large, making a census or a complete enumeration of all the values in the population impractical or impossible. The _____ represents a subset of manageable size.
   a. Dispersion
   b. Boussinesq approximation
   c. Duality
   d. Sample

7. In probability theory, the _____ or universal _____, often denoted S, Ω of an experiment or random trial is the set of all possible outcomes. For example, if the experiment is tossing a coin, the _____ is the set {head, tail}. For tossing a single six-sided die, the _____ is {1, 2, 3, 4, 5, 6}.
   a. Marginal distribution
   b. Markov chain
   c. Martingale central limit theorem
   d. Sample space

8. A _____ is a software program that facilitates symbolic mathematics. The core functionality of a CAS is manipulation of mathematical expressions in symbolic form.

Chapter 7. PROBABILITY

The symbolic manipulations supported typically include

- simplification to the smallest possible expression or some standard form, including automatic simplification with assumptions and simplification with constraints
- substitution of symbolic, functors or numeric values for expressions
- change of form of expressions: expanding products and powers, partial and full factorization, rewriting as partial fractions, constraint satisfaction, rewriting trigonometric functions as exponentials, etc.
- partial and total differentiation
- symbolic constrained and unconstrained global optimization
- solution of linear and some non-linear equations over various domains
- solution of some differential and difference equations
- taking some limits
- some indefinite and definite integration, including multidimensional integrals
- integral transforms
- arbitrary-precision numeric operations
- Series operations such as expansion, summation and products
- matrix operations including products, inverses, etc.
- display of mathematical expressions in two-dimensional mathematical form, often using typesetting systems similar to TeX
- add-ons for use in applied mathematics such as physics packages for physical computation
- plotting graphs and parametric plots of functions in two and three dimensions, and animating them
- APIs for linking it on an external program such as a database, or using in a programming language to use the _____
- drawing charts and diagrams
- string manipulation such as matching and searching
- statistical computation
- Theorem proving and verification
- graphic production and editing such as CGI and signal processing as image processing
- sound synthesis

Many also include a programming language, allowing users to implement their own algorithms.

Some _____s focus on a specific area of application; these are typically developed in academia and are free.

a. 2-3 heap
b. 120-cell
c. 1-center problem
d. Computer algebra system

9. _____ is the mathematical operation of scaling one number by another. It is one of the four basic operations in elementary arithmetic.

Chapter 7. PROBABILITY

_____ is defined for whole numbers in terms of repeated addition; for example, 4 multiplied by 3 can be calculated by adding 3 copies of 4 together:

$$4 + 4 + 4 = 12.$$

_____ of rational numbers and real numbers is defined by systematic generalization of this basic idea.

- a. Highest common factor
- b. The number 0 is even.
- c. Multiplication
- d. Least common multiple

10. In abstract algebra, a module S over a ring R is called _____ or irreducible if it is not the zero module 0 and if its only submodules are 0 and S. Understanding the _____ modules over a ring is usually helpful because these modules form the 'building blocks' of all other modules in a certain sense.

Abelian groups are the same as Z-modules.

- a. Harmonic series
- b. Basis
- c. Derivation
- d. Simple

11. In simple terms, two events are _____ if they cannot occur at the same time.

In logic, two _____ propositions are propositions that logically cannot both be true. To say that more than two propositions are _____ may, depending on context mean that no two of them can both be true, or only that they cannot all be true.

- a. Mutually exclusive
- b. Philosophy of mathematics
- c. Philosophy
- d. Determinism

12. _____ or set diagrams are diagrams that show all hypothetically possible logical relations between a finite collection of sets. _____ were invented around 1880 by John Venn. They are used in many fields, including set theory, probability, logic, statistics, and computer science.

Chapter 7. PROBABILITY

a. 120-cell
b. 2-3 heap
c. 1-center problem
d. Venn diagrams

13. A _____ is a 2D geometric symbolic representation of information according to some visualization technique. Sometimes, the technique uses a 3D visualization which is then projected onto the 2D surface. The word graph is sometimes used as a synonym for _____.
   a. 2-3 heap
   b. 1-center problem
   c. Diagram
   d. 120-cell

14. In discrete mathematics and predominantly in set theory, a _____ is a concept used in comparisons of sets to refer to the unique values of one set in relation to another. The terms 'absolute' and 'relative' _____ refer to more specific applications of the concept, with universal _____s referring to elements unique to the universal set and the latter referring to the unique elements of one set in relation to another. In this image, the universal set is represented by the border of the image, and the set A as a disc.
   a. Kernel
   b. Huge
   c. Complement
   d. Derivative algebra

15. In probability theory and statistics the _____ in favour of an event or a proposition are the quantity p /, where p is the probability of the event or proposition. The _____ against the same event are / p. For example, if you chose a random day of the week, then the _____ that you would choose a Sunday would be 1/6, not 1/7.
   a. Anscombe transform
   b. Event
   c. Estimation of covariance matrices
   d. Odds

16. _____ is the probability of some event A, given the occurrence of some other event B. _____ is written P[A | B], and is read 'the probability of A, given B'.

Joint probability is the probability of two events in conjunction. That is, it is the probability of both events together. The joint probability of A and B is written $P(A \cap B)$ or $P(A,B)$.

a. Conditional probability
b. Sample space
c. Renewal theory
d. Quantile

17. In mathematics, hyperbolic n-space, denoted H^n, is the maximally symmetric, simply connected, n-dimensional Riemannian manifold with constant sectional curvature −1. _____ is the principal example of a space exhibiting hyperbolic geometry. It can be thought of as the negative-curvature analogue of the n-sphere.
   a. Hyperbolic geometry
   b. Horocycle
   c. Margulis lemma
   d. Hyperbolic space

18. The _____ governs the differentiation of products of differentiable functions.
   a. 120-cell
   b. Reciprocal Rule
   c. 1-center problem
   d. Product rule

19. In set theory, a _____ is a partially ordered set such that for each $t \in T$, the set $\{s \in T : s < t\}$ is well-ordered by the relation <. For each $t \in T$, the order type of $\{s \in T : s < t\}$ is called the height of t. The height of T itself is the least ordinal greater than the height of each element of T.
   a. Tree
   b. Definable numbers
   c. Set-theoretic topology
   d. Transitive reduction

Chapter 8. ADDITIONAL PROBABILITY Topics

1. In mathematics, a _____, named after Andrey Markov, is a stochastic process with the Markov property. Having the Markov property means that, given the present state, future states are independent of the past states. In other words, the description of the present state fully captures all the information that could influence the future evolution of the process. Future states will be reached through a probabilistic process instead of a deterministic one.

   a. Variance-to-mean ratio
   b. Law of Truly Large Numbers
   c. Possibility theory
   d. Markov chain

2. A _____ is a software program that facilitates symbolic mathematics. The core functionality of a CAS is manipulation of mathematical expressions in symbolic form.

The symbolic manipulations supported typically include

- simplification to the smallest possible expression or some standard form, including automatic simplification with assumptions and simplification with constraints
- substitution of symbolic, functors or numeric values for expressions
- change of form of expressions: expanding products and powers, partial and full factorization, rewriting as partial fractions, constraint satisfaction, rewriting trigonometric functions as exponentials, etc.
- partial and total differentiation
- symbolic constrained and unconstrained global optimization
- solution of linear and some non-linear equations over various domains
- solution of some differential and difference equations
- taking some limits
- some indefinite and definite integration, including multidimensional integrals
- integral transforms
- arbitrary-precision numeric operations
- Series operations such as expansion, summation and products
- matrix operations including products, inverses, etc.
- display of mathematical expressions in two-dimensional mathematical form, often using typesetting systems similar to TeX
- add-ons for use in applied mathematics such as physics packages for physical computation
- plotting graphs and parametric plots of functions in two and three dimensions, and animating them
- APIs for linking it on an external program such as a database, or using in a programming language to use the _____
- drawing charts and diagrams
- string manipulation such as matching and searching
- statistical computation
- Theorem proving and verification
- graphic production and editing such as CGI and signal processing as image processing
- sound synthesis

Many also include a programming language, allowing users to implement their own algorithms.

Some _____s focus on a specific area of application; these are typically developed in academia and are free.

a. 120-cell
b. 1-center problem
c. 2-3 heap
d. Computer algebra system

3. In mathematics and in the sciences, a _____ (plural: _____e, formulæ or _____s) is a concise way of expressing information symbolically (as in a mathematical or chemical _____), or a general relationship between quantities. One of many famous _____e is Albert Einstein's E = mc² (see special relativity

In mathematics, a _____ is a key to solve an equation with variables. For example, the problem of determining the volume of a sphere is one that requires a significant amount of integral calculus to solve.

a. 120-cell
b. Formula
c. 2-3 heap
d. 1-center problem

4. In number theory, a _____ of a positive integer n is a way of writing n as a sum of positive integers. Two sums which only differ in the order of their summands are considered to be the same _____; if order matters then the sum becomes a composition. A summand in a _____ is also called a part.
a. Distribution
b. Congruent
c. Derivative algebra
d. Partition

5. In mathematics, hyperbolic n-space, denoted H^n, is the maximally symmetric, simply connected, n-dimensional Riemannian manifold with constant sectional curvature −1. _____ is the principal example of a space exhibiting hyperbolic geometry. It can be thought of as the negative-curvature analogue of the n-sphere.
a. Margulis lemma
b. Horocycle
c. Hyperbolic geometry
d. Hyperbolic space

Chapter 8. ADDITIONAL PROBABILITY Topics

6. In engineering and manufacturing, _____ is involved in developing systems to ensure products or services are designed and produced to meet or exceed customer requirements or SLA's. Genetic algorithms are search techniques, used in computing to find exact or approximate solutions to optimization and search problems.

Alternative _____ procedures can be applied on a process to test statistically the null hypothesis, that the process is in control, against the alternative, that the process is out of control.

   a. Statistical process control
   b. 120-cell
   c. 1-center problem
   d. Quality control

7. The terms 'a priori' and '_____' are used in philosophy to distinguish two types of knowledge, justifications or arguments. A priori knowledge or justification is independent of experience; _____ knowledge or justification is dependent on experience or empirical evidence. A priori justification makes no reference to experience; the issue concerns how one knows the proposition or claim in question--what justifies or grounds one's belief in it.
   a. A posteriori
   b. A Mathematical Theory of Communication
   c. A chemical equation
   d. A posteriori

8. In statistics, _____ knowledge refers to prior knowledge about a population, rather than that estimated by recent observation. It is common in Bayesian inference to make inferences conditional upon this knowledge, and the integration of _____ knowledge is the central difference between the Bayesian and Frequentist approach to statistics. We need not be 100% certain about something before it can be considered _____ knowledge, but conducting estimation conditional upon assumptions for which there is little evidence should be avoided.
   a. ARIA
   b. Imputation
   c. Interval
   d. A priori

9. Introduction

In the theory of probability and statistics, a _____ is an experiment whose outcome is random and can be either of two possible outcomes, 'success' and 'failure'.

In practice it refers to a single experiment which can have one of two possible outcomes. These events can be phrased into 'yes or no' questions:

- Did the coin land heads?
- Was the newborn child a girl?
- Were a person's eyes green?
- Did a mosquito die after the area was sprayed with insecticide?
- Did a potential customer decide to buy a product?
- Did a citizen vote for a specific candidate?
- Did an employee vote pro-union?

Therefore success and failure are labels for outcomes, and should not be construed literally. Examples of _____s include

- Flipping a coin. In this context, obverse conventionally denotes success and reverse denotes failure. A fair coin has the probability of success 0.5 by definition.
- Rolling a die, where a six is 'success' and everything else a 'failure'.
- In conducting a political opinion poll, choosing a voter at random to ascertain whether that voter will vote 'yes' in an upcoming referendum.

Mathematically, a _____ can be described by a sample space Ω consisting of two values, s for 'success' and f for 'failure'. Therefore the sample space is $\Omega = \{s, f\}$.

a. Point process
b. Bernoulli trial
c. Law of total cumulance
d. Marginal distribution

10. In elementary algebra, a _____ is a polynomial with two terms: the sum of two monomials. It is the simplest kind of polynomial except for a monomial.

The _____ $a^2 - b^2$ can be factored as the product of two other _____s:

$a^2 - b^2$.

The product of a pair of linear _____s a x + b and c x + d is:

2 +x + bd.

Chapter 8. ADDITIONAL PROBABILITY Topics

A _____ raised to the nth power, represented as

n

can be expanded by means of the _____ theorem or, equivalently, using Pascal's triangle.

   a. Real structure
   b. Binomial
   c. Rational root theorem
   d. Cylindrical algebraic decomposition

11. _____ typically deals with the probability of several successive decisions, each of which has two possible outcomes.

The probability of an event can be expressed as a _____ if its outcomes can be broken down into two probabilities p and q, where p and q are complementary For example, tossing a coin can be either heads or tails, each which have a probability of 0.5. Rolling a four on a six-sided die can be expressed as the probability of getting a 4 or the probability of rolling something else.

   a. Marginal distribution
   b. Binomial probability
   c. Markov chain
   d. Quantile

12. _____ is the likelihood or chance that something is the case or will happen. Theoretical _____ is used extensively in areas such as statistics, mathematics, science and philosophy to draw conclusions about the likelihood of potential events and the underlying mechanics of complex systems.

The word _____ does not have a consistent direct definition.

   a. Discrete random variable
   b. Statistical significance
   c. Standardized moment
   d. Probability

13. In probability theory and statistics, the _____ of a random variable is the integral of the random variable with respect to its probability measure. For discrete random variables this is equivalent to the probability-weighted sum of the possible values, and for continuous random variables with a density function it is the probability density -weighted integral of the possible values.

The _____ may be intuitively understood by the law of large numbers: The _____, when it exists, is almost surely the limit of the sample mean as sample size grows to infinity.

a. Illustration
b. Infinitely divisible distribution
c. Event
d. Expected value

14. _____ is a general term for any type of information processing. This includes phenomena ranging from human thinking to calculations with a more narrow meaning. _____ is a process following a well-defined model that is understood and can be expressed in an algorithm, protocol, network topology, etc.

a. 1-center problem
b. 120-cell
c. 2-3 heap
d. Computation

15. _____ in North America, South Africa and Australia, and Operational Research in Europe, is an interdisciplinary branch of applied mathematics and formal science that uses methods such as mathematical modeling, statistics, and algorithms to arrive at optimal or near optimal solutions to complex problems. It is typically concerned with optimizing the maxima or minima of some objective function. _____ helps management achieve its goals using scientific methods.

a. A Mathematical Theory of Communication
b. A chemical equation
c. A posteriori
d. Operations research

16. In mathematics, _____ are used in the study of chance and probability. They were developed to assist in the analysis of games of chance, stochastic events, and the results of scientific experiments by capturing only the mathematical properties necessary to answer probabilistic questions. Further formalizations have firmly grounded the entity in the theoretical domains of mathematics by making use of measure theory.

a. Median polish
b. Random variables
c. Statistics
d. Statistical dispersion

17. In differential geometry, a discipline within mathematics, a _____ is a subset of the tangent bundle of a manifold satisfying certain properties. _____s are used to build up notions of integrability, and specifically of a foliation of a manifold
    a. Constraint
    b. Distribution
    c. Coherence
    d. Discontinuity

Chapter 9. STATISTICS

1. In probability theory, a probability distribution is called _____ if its cumulative distribution function is _____. That is equivalent to saying that for random variables X with the distribution in question, Pr[X = a] = 0 for all real numbers a. If the distribution of X is _____ then X is called a _____ random variable.
    a. Concatenated codes
    b. Continuous
    c. Conull set
    d. Continuous phase modulation

2. A _____ is the result of applying a function to a set of data.

More formally, statistical theory defines a _____ as a function of a sample where the function itself is independent of the sample's distribution: the term is used both for the function and for the value of the function on a given sample.

A _____ is distinct from an unknown statistical parameter, which is not computable from a sample.

    a. Statistic
    b. Parameter space
    c. Spatial dependence
    d. Loss function

3. _____ is a mathematical science pertaining to the collection, analysis, interpretation or explanation, and presentation of data. It also provides tools for prediction and forecasting based on data. It is applicable to a wide variety of academic disciplines, from the natural and social sciences to the humanities, government and business.
    a. Percentile rank
    b. Regression toward the mean
    c. Probability distribution
    d. Statistics

4. A _____ is a statistical sample of a population in which some members of the population are less likely to be included than others. If the bias makes estimation of population parameters impossible, the sample is a non-probability sample.

An extreme form of biased sampling occurs when certain members of the population are totally excluded from the sample.

a. Biased sample
b. Proof by verbosity
c. Correlation does not imply causation
d. Spurious relationship

5. A sample is a subject chosen from a population for investigation. A _____ is one chosen by a method involving an unpredictable component. Random sampling can also refer to taking a number of independent observations from the same probability distribution, without involving any real population.
    a. Selection bias
    b. Randomized response
    c. Random sample
    d. Systematic sampling

6. In statistics, a _____ is a subset of a population. Typically, the population is very large, making a census or a complete enumeration of all the values in the population impractical or impossible. The _____ represents a subset of manageable size.
    a. Boussinesq approximation
    b. Sample
    c. Duality
    d. Dispersion

7. _____ is the act or process of deriving a conclusion based solely on what one knows.

   _____ is studied within several different fields.

   - Human _____ is traditionally studied within the field of cognitive psychology.
   - Logic studies the laws of valid _____.
   - Statisticians have developed formal rules for _____ from quantitative data.
   - Artificial intelligence researchers develop automated _____ systems.

The process by which a conclusion is inferred from multiple observations is called inductive reasoning. The conclusion may be correct or incorrect, or partially correct, or correct to within a certain degree of accuracy, or correct in certain situations.

   a. Inference
   b. A posteriori
   c. A Mathematical Theory of Communication
   d. A chemical equation

8. In mathematics, a _____ is a statement that can be proved on the basis of explicitly stated or previously agreed assumptions.
   a. Disjunction introduction
   b. Boolean function
   c. Logical value
   d. Theorem

9. A bar chart or _____ is a chart with rectangular bars with lengths proportional to the values that they represent. Bar charts are used for comparing two or more values. The bars can be horizontally or vertically oriented.
   a. 120-cell
   b. 2-3 heap
   c. 1-center problem
   d. Bar graph

10. A _____ is a circular chart divided into sectors, illustrating relative magnitudes or frequences or percents. In a _____, the arc length of each sector, is proportional to the quantity it represents. Together, the sectors create a full disk.
    a. 2-3 heap
    b. 1-center problem
    c. 120-cell
    d. Pie chart

11. In statistics the _____ of an event i is the number n_i of times the event occurred in the experiment or the study. These frequencies are often graphically represented in histograms.

We speak of absolute frequencies, when the counts n_i themselves are given and of

$$f_i = \frac{n_i}{N} = \frac{n_i}{\sum_i n_i}$$

Taking the f_i for all i and tabulating or plotting them leads to a _____ distribution.

   a. Robinson-Dadson curves
   b. Digital room correction
   c. Frequency
   d. Subharmonic

12. A _____ or line graph is a type of graph created by connecting a series of data points together with a line.

A _____ is a basic type of chart common in many fields. It is an extension of a scatter graph, and is created by connecting a series of points that represent individual measurements with line segments.

a. Line chart
b. 120-cell
c. 2-3 heap
d. 1-center problem

13. In set theory and its applications throughout mathematics, a _____ is a collection of sets that can be unambiguously defined by a property that all its members share. The precise definition of '_____' depends on foundational context. In work on ZF set theory, the notion of _____ is informal, whereas other set theories, such as NBG set theory, axiomatize the notion of '_____'.
a. Congruent
b. Class
c. Coherence
d. Filter

14. In descriptive statistics, the _____ is the length of the smallest interval which contains all the data. It is calculated by subtracting the smallest observations from the greatest and provides an indication of statistical dispersion.

It is measured in the same units as the data.

a. Class
b. Bandwidth
c. Range
d. Kernel

15. In mathematics, a _____ is a set of real numbers with the property that any number that lies between two numbers in the set is also included in the set. For example, the set of all numbers x satisfying $0 \leq x \leq 1$ is an _____ which contains 0 and 1, as well as all numbers between them. Other examples of _____s are the set of all real numbers $\mathbb{R}$, the set of all positive real numbers, and the empty set.
a. Annihilator
b. Interval
c. Ideal
d. Order

Chapter 9. STATISTICS

16. In mathematics, the concept of a '_____' is used to describe the behavior of a function as its argument or input either 'gets close' to some point, or as the argument becomes arbitrarily large; or the behavior of a sequence's elements as their index increases indefinitely. _____s are used in calculus and other branches of mathematical analysis to define derivatives and continuity.

In formulas, _____ is usually abbreviated as lim.

   a. Duality
   b. Copula
   c. Contact
   d. Limit

17. In statistics, a _____ is a graphical display of tabulated frequencies, shown as bars. It shows what proportion of cases fall into each of several categories. A _____ differs from a bar chart in that it is the area of the bar that denotes the value, not the height as in bar charts, a crucial distinction when the categories are not of uniform width.
   a. Probability distribution
   b. Standardized moment
   c. First-hitting-time models
   d. Histogram

18. In geometry a _____ is traditionally a plane figure that is bounded by a closed path or circuit, composed of a finite sequence of straight line segments. These segments are called its edges or sides, and the points where two edges meet are the _____'s vertices or corners. The interior of the _____ is sometimes called its body.
   a. Regular polygon
   b. Polygonal curve
   c. Parallelogon
   d. Polygon

19. In differential geometry, a discipline within mathematics, a _____ is a subset of the tangent bundle of a manifold satisfying certain properties. _____s are used to build up notions of integrability, and specifically of a foliation of a manifold
   a. Coherence
   b. Distribution
   c. Discontinuity
   d. Constraint

Chapter 9. STATISTICS

20. In statistics, a _____ is a list of the values that a variable takes in a sample. It is usually a list, ordered by quantity, showing the number of times each value appears. For example, if 100 people rate a five-point Likert scale assessing their agreement with a statement on a scale on which 1 denotes strong agreement and 5 strong disagreement, the _____ of their responses might look like:

This simple tabulation has two drawbacks.

   a. Confounding
   b. Frequency distribution
   c. Covariance
   d. Percentile

21. In mathematics and statistics, the _____ of a list of numbers is the sum of all of the list divided by the number of items in the list. If the list is a statistical population, then the mean of that population is called a population mean. If the list is a statistical sample, we call the resulting statistic a sample mean.
   a. Interval estimation
   b. Unsolved problems in statistics
   c. Analysis of variance
   d. Arithmetic mean

22. In mathematics, an average, or _____ of a data set refers to a measure of the 'middle' or 'expected' value of the data set. There are many different descriptive statistics that can be chosen as a measurement of the _____ of the data items.

An average is a single value that is meant to typify a list of values.

   a. Mean reciprocal rank
   b. Quartile
   c. Central tendency
   d. Trimean

23. In statistics, _____ has two related meanings:

   • the arithmetic _____.
   • the expected value of a random variable, which is also called the population _____.

It is sometimes stated that the '_____' _____s average. This is incorrect if '_____' is taken in the specific sense of 'arithmetic _____' as there are different types of averages: the _____, median, and mode. For instance, average house prices almost always use the median value for the average.

For a real-valued random variable X, the _____ is the expectation of X.

a. Probability
b. Proportional hazards model
c. Mean
d. Statistical population

24. In mathematics the concept of a _____ generalizes notions such as 'length', 'area', and 'volume'. Informally, given some base set, a '_____' is any consistent assignment of 'sizes' to the subsets of the base set. Depending on the application, the 'size' of a subset may be interpreted as its physical size, the amount of something that lies within the subset, or the probability that some random process will yield a result within the subset.

a. Measure
b. Lattice
c. Cusp
d. Congruent

25. In geometry, a _____ of a triangle is a line segment joining a vertex to the midpoint of the opposing side. Every triangle has exactly three _____s; one running from each vertex to the opposite side.

The three _____s are concurrent at a point known as the triangle's centroid, or center of mass of the triangle.

a. Median
b. Statistical significance
c. Correlation
d. Percentile rank

26. _____ is a method of constructing new data points from a discrete set of known data points.
a. Integration by substitution
b. Interpolation
c. Archimedes' use of infinitesimals
d. Uniform convergence

27. A _____ is the value of a variable below which a certain percent of observations fall. So the 20th _____ is the value below which 20 percent of the observations may be found. The term _____ and the related term _____ rank are often used in descriptive statistics as well as in the reporting of scores from norm-referenced tests.

Chapter 9. STATISTICS

a. Statistically significant
b. Logistic regression
c. Frequency distribution
d. Percentile

28. In statistics, the _____ is the value that occurs the most frequently in a data set or a probability distribution. In some fields, notably education, sample data are often called scores, and the sample _____ is known as the modal score.

Like the statistical mean and the median, the _____ is a way of capturing important information about a random variable or a population in a single quantity.

a. Field
b. Function
c. Deltoid
d. Mode

29. _____ and sample covariance are statistics computed from a collection of data, thought of as being random.

Given a random sample $X_1, \ldots, X_N$ from an n-dimensional random variable X, the _____ is

$$\bar{X} = \frac{1}{N} \sum_{k=1}^{N} X_k.$$

In coordinates, writing the vectors as columns,

$$X_k = \begin{bmatrix} x_{1k} \\ \vdots \\ x_{nk} \end{bmatrix}, \quad \bar{X} = \begin{bmatrix} \bar{x}_1 \\ \vdots \\ \bar{x}_n \end{bmatrix},$$

the entries of the _____ are

$$\bar{x}_i = \frac{1}{N} \sum_{k=1}^{N} x_{ik}, \quad i = 1, \ldots, n.$$

The sample covariance of $X_1, \ldots, X_N$ is the n-by-n matrix $Q = [q_{ij}]$ with the entries given by

$$q_{ij} = \frac{1}{N-1} \sum_{k=1}^{N} (x_{ik} - \bar{x}_i)(x_{jk} - \bar{x}_j)$$

The _____ and the sample covariance matrix are unbiased estimates of the mean and the covariance matrix of the random variable X. The reason why the sample covariance matrix has $N-1$ in the denominator rather than N is essentially that the population mean E is not known and is replaced by the _____ $\bar{x}$.

a. Sample mean
b. Mathematical statistics
c. Skewness
d. Covariance

30. In optics, _____ is the phenomenon in which the phase velocity of a wave depends on its frequency. Media having such a property are termed dispersive media.

The most familiar example of _____ is probably a rainbow, in which _____ causes the spatial separation of a white light into components of different wavelengths.

a. Crib
b. Dispersion
c. Depth
d. Boussinesq approximation

31. In probability theory and statistics, the _____ of a random variable, probability distribution averaging the squared distance of its possible values from the expected value. Whereas the mean is a way to describe the location of a distribution, the _____ is a way to capture its scale or degree of being spread out. The unit of _____ is the square of the unit of the original variable.

a. Kendall tau rank correlation coefficient
b. Probability distribution
c. Nonlinear regression
d. Variance

32. In probability and statistics, the _____ is a measure of the dispersion of a collection of numbers. It can apply to a probability distribution, a random variable, a population or a data set. The _____ is usually denoted with the letter σ.

a. Null hypothesis
b. Standard deviation
c. Statistical population
d. Failure rate

33. In mathematics and statistics, _____ is a measure of difference for interval and ratio variables between the observed value and the mean. The sign of _____, either positive or negative, indicates whether the observation is larger than or smaller than the mean. The magnitude of the value reports how different an observation is from the mean.
   a. Conchoid
   b. Functional
   c. Filter
   d. Deviation

34. In mathematics, specifically in combinatorial commutative algebra, a convex lattice polytope P is called _____ if it has the following property: given any positive integer n, every lattice point of the dilation nP, obtained from P by scaling its vertices by the factor n and taking the convex hull of the resulting points, can be written as the sum of exactly n lattice points in P. This property plays an important role in the theory of toric varieties, where it corresponds to projective normality of the toric variety determined by P.

The simplex in R^k with the vertices at the origin and along the unit coordinate vectors is _____.

   a. Demihypercubes
   b. Hypercube
   c. Polytetrahedron
   d. Normal

35. The _____ is an important family of continuous probability distributions, applicable in many fields. Each member of the family may be defined by two parameters, location and scale: the mean and variance respectively. The standard _____ is the _____ with a mean of zero and a variance of one.
   a. Null hypothesis
   b. Percentile rank
   c. Normal distribution
   d. Coefficient of variation

36. In mathematics, the concept of a _____ tries to capture the intuitive idea of a geometrical one-dimensional and continuous object. A simple example is the circle. In everyday use of the term '_____', a straight line is not curved, but in mathematical parlance _____s include straight lines and line segments.

a. Kappa curve
b. Curve
c. Quadrifolium
d. Negative pedal curve

37. In mathematics, hyperbolic n-space, denoted H^n, is the maximally symmetric, simply connected, n-dimensional Riemannian manifold with constant sectional curvature −1. _____ is the principal example of a space exhibiting hyperbolic geometry. It can be thought of as the negative-curvature analogue of the n-sphere.

a. Margulis lemma
b. Horocycle
c. Hyperbolic space
d. Hyperbolic geometry

38. In elementary algebra, a _____ is a polynomial with two terms: the sum of two monomials. It is the simplest kind of polynomial except for a monomial.

The _____ $a^2 - b^2$ can be factored as the product of two other _____s:

$a^2 - b^2$.

The product of a pair of linear _____s a x + b and c x + d is:

2 +x + bd.

A _____ raised to the nth power, represented as

n

can be expanded by means of the _____ theorem or, equivalently, using Pascal's triangle.

a. Real structure
b. Cylindrical algebraic decomposition
c. Rational root theorem
d. Binomial

39. _____ typically deals with the probability of several successive decisions, each of which has two possible outcomes.

The probability of an event can be expressed as a _____ if its outcomes can be broken down into two probabilities p and q, where p and q are complementary For example, tossing a coin can be either heads or tails, each which have a probability of 0.5. Rolling a four on a six-sided die can be expressed as the probability of getting a 4 or the probability of rolling something else.

a. Quantile
b. Binomial probability
c. Marginal distribution
d. Markov chain

40. In mathematics, a _____, named after Andrey Markov, is a stochastic process with the Markov property. Having the Markov property means that, given the present state, future states are independent of the past states. In other words, the description of the present state fully captures all the information that could influence the future evolution of the process. Future states will be reached through a probabilistic process instead of a deterministic one.

a. Variance-to-mean ratio
b. Possibility theory
c. Markov chain
d. Law of Truly Large Numbers

41. A _____ is a software program that facilitates symbolic mathematics. The core functionality of a CAS is manipulation of mathematical expressions in symbolic form.

The symbolic manipulations supported typically include

- simplification to the smallest possible expression or some standard form, including automatic simplification with assumptions and simplification with constraints
- substitution of symbolic, functors or numeric values for expressions
- change of form of expressions: expanding products and powers, partial and full factorization, rewriting as partial fractions, constraint satisfaction, rewriting trigonometric functions as exponentials, etc.
- partial and total differentiation
- symbolic constrained and unconstrained global optimization
- solution of linear and some non-linear equations over various domains
- solution of some differential and difference equations
- taking some limits
- some indefinite and definite integration, including multidimensional integrals
- integral transforms
- arbitrary-precision numeric operations
- Series operations such as expansion, summation and products
- matrix operations including products, inverses, etc.
- display of mathematical expressions in two-dimensional mathematical form, often using typesetting systems similar to TeX
- add-ons for use in applied mathematics such as physics packages for physical computation
- plotting graphs and parametric plots of functions in two and three dimensions, and animating them
- APIs for linking it on an external program such as a database, or using in a programming language to use the _____
- drawing charts and diagrams
- string manipulation such as matching and searching
- statistical computation
- Theorem proving and verification
- graphic production and editing such as CGI and signal processing as image processing
- sound synthesis

Many also include a programming language, allowing users to implement their own algorithms.

Some _____s focus on a specific area of application; these are typically developed in academia and are free.

a. 2-3 heap
b. Computer algebra system
c. 1-center problem
d. 120-cell

42. _____ is the likelihood or chance that something is the case or will happen. Theoretical _____ is used extensively in areas such as statistics, mathematics, science and philosophy to draw conclusions about the likelihood of potential events and the underlying mechanics of complex systems.

The word _____ does not have a consistent direct definition.

a. Probability
b. Statistical significance
c. Standardized moment
d. Discrete random variable

43. In engineering and manufacturing, _____ is involved in developing systems to ensure products or services are designed and produced to meet or exceed customer requirements or SLA's. Genetic algorithms are search techniques, used in computing to find exact or approximate solutions to optimization and search problems.

Alternative _____ procedures can be applied on a process to test statistically the null hypothesis, that the process is in control, against the alternative, that the process is out of control.

a. Statistical process control
b. Quality control
c. 120-cell
d. 1-center problem

Chapter 10. MARKOV CHAINS; GAMES

1. Introduction

In the theory of probability and statistics, a _____ is an experiment whose outcome is random and can be either of two possible outcomes, 'success' and 'failure'.

In practice it refers to a single experiment which can have one of two possible outcomes. These events can be phrased into 'yes or no' questions:

- Did the coin land heads?
- Was the newborn child a girl?
- Were a person's eyes green?
- Did a mosquito die after the area was sprayed with insecticide?
- Did a potential customer decide to buy a product?
- Did a citizen vote for a specific candidate?
- Did an employee vote pro-union?

Therefore success and failure are labels for outcomes, and should not be construed literally. Examples of _____ s include

- Flipping a coin. In this context, obverse conventionally denotes success and reverse denotes failure. A fair coin has the probability of success 0.5 by definition.
- Rolling a die, where a six is 'success' and everything else a 'failure'.
- In conducting a political opinion poll, choosing a voter at random to ascertain whether that voter will vote 'yes' in an upcoming referendum.

Mathematically, a _____ can be described by a sample space Ω consisting of two values, s for 'success' and f for 'failure'. Therefore the sample space is $\Omega = \{s, f\}$.

a. Law of total cumulance
b. Point process
c. Marginal distribution
d. Bernoulli trial

2. In mathematics, a _____, named after Andrey Markov, is a stochastic process with the Markov property. Having the Markov property means that, given the present state, future states are independent of the past states. In other words, the description of the present state fully captures all the information that could influence the future evolution of the process. Future states will be reached through a probabilistic process instead of a deterministic one.

a. Markov chain
b. Possibility theory
c. Law of Truly Large Numbers
d. Variance-to-mean ratio

3. In mathematics, a _____ is a rectangular table of elements, which may be numbers or, more generally, any abstract quantities that can be added and multiplied. Matrices are used to describe linear equations, keep track of the coefficients of linear transformations and to record data that depend on multiple parameters. Matrices are described by the field of _____ theory.
   a. Double counting
   b. Coherent
   c. Compression
   d. Matrix

4. In mathematics, a stochastic matrix, probability matrix, or _____ is used to describe the transitions of a Markov chain. It has found use in probability theory, statistics and linear algebra, as well as computer science. There are several different definitions and types of stochastic matrices;

   A right stochastic matrix is a square matrix each of whose rows consists of nonnegative real numbers, with each row summing to 1.

   a. Pick matrix
   b. Sylvester matrix
   c. Hessenberg matrix
   d. Transition matrix

5. In ecology, predation describes a biological interaction where a _____ (an organism that is hunting) feeds on its prey, the organism that is attacked. _____s may or may not kill their prey prior to feeding on them, but the act of predation always results in the death of the prey. The other main category of consumption is detritivory, the consumption of dead organic material (detritus.)
   a. 120-cell
   b. Prey
   c. 1-center problem
   d. Predator

6. Initial objects are also called _____, and terminal objects are also called final.
   a. Direct limit
   b. Colimit
   c. Terminal object
   d. Coterminal

7. A _____ is a software program that facilitates symbolic mathematics. The core functionality of a CAS is manipulation of mathematical expressions in symbolic form.

Chapter 10. MARKOV CHAINS; GAMES

The symbolic manipulations supported typically include

- simplification to the smallest possible expression or some standard form, including automatic simplification with assumptions and simplification with constraints
- substitution of symbolic, functors or numeric values for expressions
- change of form of expressions: expanding products and powers, partial and full factorization, rewriting as partial fractions, constraint satisfaction, rewriting trigonometric functions as exponentials, etc.
- partial and total differentiation
- symbolic constrained and unconstrained global optimization
- solution of linear and some non-linear equations over various domains
- solution of some differential and difference equations
- taking some limits
- some indefinite and definite integration, including multidimensional integrals
- integral transforms
- arbitrary-precision numeric operations
- Series operations such as expansion, summation and products
- matrix operations including products, inverses, etc.
- display of mathematical expressions in two-dimensional mathematical form, often using typesetting systems similar to TeX
- add-ons for use in applied mathematics such as physics packages for physical computation
- plotting graphs and parametric plots of functions in two and three dimensions, and animating them
- APIs for linking it on an external program such as a database, or using in a programming language to use the _____
- drawing charts and diagrams
- string manipulation such as matching and searching
- statistical computation
- Theorem proving and verification
- graphic production and editing such as CGI and signal processing as image processing
- sound synthesis

Many also include a programming language, allowing users to implement their own algorithms.

Some _____s focus on a specific area of application; these are typically developed in academia and are free.

a. 120-cell
b. 2-3 heap
c. 1-center problem
d. Computer algebra system

Chapter 10. MARKOV CHAINS; GAMES

8. In differential geometry, a discipline within mathematics, a _____ is a subset of the tangent bundle of a manifold satisfying certain properties. _____s are used to build up notions of integrability, and specifically of a foliation of a manifold
   a. Distribution
   b. Discontinuity
   c. Constraint
   d. Coherence

9. _____ is the likelihood or chance that something is the case or will happen. Theoretical _____ is used extensively in areas such as statistics, mathematics, science and philosophy to draw conclusions about the likelihood of potential events and the underlying mechanics of complex systems.

The word _____ does not have a consistent direct definition.

   a. Standardized moment
   b. Probability
   c. Discrete random variable
   d. Statistical significance

10. In probability theory and statistics, a _____ identifies either the probability of each value of an unidentified random variable, or the probability of the value falling within a particular interval. The probability function describes the range of possible values that a random variable can attain and the probability that the value of the random variable is within any subset of that range.

When the random variable takes values in the set of real numbers, the _____ is completely described by the cumulative distribution function, whose value at each real x is the probability that the random variable is smaller than or equal to x.

   a. Normal distribution
   b. Statistical graphics
   c. Z-test
   d. Probability distribution

11. In physics and in _____ calculus, a _____ is a concept characterized by a magnitude and a direction. A _____ can be thought of as an arrow in Euclidean space, drawn from an initial point A pointing to a terminal point B.

a. Dominance
b. Deviation
c. Constraint
d. Vector

12. In mathematics, hyperbolic n-space, denoted H^n, is the maximally symmetric, simply connected, n-dimensional Riemannian manifold with constant sectional curvature −1. _____ is the principal example of a space exhibiting hyperbolic geometry. It can be thought of as the negative-curvature analogue of the n-sphere.
    a. Hyperbolic geometry
    b. Margulis lemma
    c. Hyperbolic space
    d. Horocycle

13. A _____ is a structured activity, usually undertaken for enjoyment and sometimes also used as an educational tool. _____s are distinct from work, which is usually carried out for remuneration, and from art, which is more concerned with the expression of ideas. However, the distinction is not clear-cut, and many _____s are also considered to be work (such as professional players of spectator sports/_____s) or art (such as jigsaw puzzles or _____s involving an artistic layout such as Mah-jongg solitaire.)
    a. 1-center problem
    b. 2-3 heap
    c. 120-cell
    d. Game

14. The word _____ has many distinct meanings in different fields of knowledge, depending on their methodologies and the context of discussion. Broadly speaking we can say that a _____ is some kind of belief or claim that (supposedly) explains, asserts, or consolidates some class of claims. Additionally, in contrast with a theorem the statement of the _____ is generally accepted only in some tentative fashion as opposed to regarding it as having been conclusively established.
    a. Defined
    b. Per mil
    c. Transport of structure
    d. Theory

15. _____ is a branch of applied mathematics that is used in the social sciences, biology, engineering, political science, international relations, computer science, and philosophy. _____ attempts to mathematically capture behavior in strategic situations, in which an individual's success in making choices depends on the choices of others. While initially developed to analyze competitions in which one individual does better at another's expense, it has been expanded to treat a wide class of interactions, which are classified according to several criteria.

a. Consumer theory
b. Mathematical economics
c. Computational economic
d. Game theory

16. In game theory, a player's _____ in a game is a complete plan of action for whatever situation might arise; this fully determines the player's behaviour. A player's _____ will determine the action the player will take at any stage of the game, for every possible history of play up to that stage.

A _____ profile is a set of strategies for each player which fully specifies all actions in a game.

a. Matching pennies
b. Strategy
c. Sir Philip Sidney game
d. Correlated equilibrium

17. In mathematics, a _____ is a point in the domain of a function of two variables which is a stationary point but not a local extremum. At such a point, in general, the surface resembles a saddle that curves up in one direction, and curves down in a different direction. In terms of contour lines, a _____ can be recognized, in general, by a contour that appears to intersect itself.

a. 1-center problem
b. Gauss map
c. Saddle point
d. Gauss-Codazzi equations

18. _____ was a Hungarian American mathematician who made major contributions to a vast range of fields, including set theory, functional analysis, quantum mechanics, ergodic theory, continuous geometry, economics and game theory, computer science, numerical analysis, hydrodynamics, and statistics, as well as many other mathematical fields. He is generally regarded as one of the foremost mathematicians of the 20th century. The mathematician Jean Dieudonné called von Neumann 'the last of the great mathematicians.' Most notably, von Neumann was a pioneer of the application of operator theory to quantum mechanics, a principal member of the Manhattan Project and the Institute for Advanced Study in Princeton, and a key figure in the development of game theory and the concepts of cellular automata and the universal constructor.

a. Frederick William Winterbotham
b. John von Neumann
c. Stuart Milner-Barry
d. Hemachandra Surī

19. In geometry, a _____ is defined as a quadrilateral where all four of its angles are right angles.

a. Polytope
b. Rectangle
c. Cantor-Dedekind axiom
d. Point group in two dimensions

Chapter 11. LOGIC

1. _____ is the study of the principles of valid demonstration and inference. _____ is a branch of philosophy, a part of the classical trivium of grammar, _____, and rhetoric. of λογικÏŒς, 'possessed of reason, intellectual, dialectical, argumentative', from λÏŒγος logos, 'word, thought, idea, argument, account, reason, or principle'.

   a. Logic
   b. Satisfiability
   c. Boolean function
   d. Counterpart theory

2. In logic and philosophy, _____ refers to either (a) the 'content' or 'meaning' of a meaningful declarative sentence or (b) the pattern of symbols, marks, or sounds that make up a meaningful declarative sentence. _____s in either case are intended to be truth-bearers, that is, they are either true or false.

   The existence of _____s in the former sense, as well as the existence of 'meanings', is disputed.

   a. Laws of classical logic
   b. Linear logic
   c. Logicism
   d. Proposition

3. In logic and mathematics, or, also known as logical _____ or inclusive _____ is a logical operator that results in true whenever one or more of its operands are true. In grammar, or is a coordinating conjunction. In ordinary language 'or' rather has the meaning of exclusive _____.

   a. Triquetra
   b. Cube
   c. Zero-point energy
   d. Disjunction

4. In logic and mathematics, _____ or not is an operation on logical values, for example, the logical value of a proposition, that sends true to false and false to true. Intuitively, the _____ of a proposition holds exactly when that proposition does not hold. In grammar, nor is an adverb which acts as a coordinating conjunction.

   a. 1-center problem
   b. Sentence diagram
   c. Syntax
   d. Negation

5. A _____ is a mathematical table used in logic -- specifically in connection with Boolean algebra, boolean functions, and propositional calculus -- to compute the functional values of logical expressions on each of their functional arguments, that is, on each combination of values taken by their logical variables. In particular, _____s can be used to tell whether a propositional expression is true for all legitimate input values, that is, logically valid.

Chapter 11. LOGIC

The pattern of reasoning that the _____ tabulates was Frege's, Peirce's, and Schröder's by 1880.

a. 120-cell
b. Truth table
c. 1-center problem
d. 2-3 heap

6. A _____ is an algebraic equation in which each term is either a constant or the product of a constant and a single variable. _____s can have one, two, three or more variables.

_____s occur with great regularity in applied mathematics.

a. Difference of two squares
b. Quartic equation
c. Linear equation
d. Quadratic equation

7. _____ In logic, statements p and q are logically equivalent if they have the same logical content.
a. Realizability
b. Logical equivalence
c. Fallacies of definition
d. Distribution rule

8. _____ describes the property of operations in mathematics and computer science which means that multiple applications of the operation does not change the result. The concept of _____ arises in a number of places in abstract algebra.

There are several meanings of _____, depending on what the concept is applied to:

- A unary operation is called idempotent if, whenever it is applied twice to any value, it gives the same result as if it were applied once. For example, the absolute value function is idempotent as a function from the set of real numbers to the set of real numbers: ab = ab.
- A binary operation is called idempotent if, whenever it is applied to two equal values, it gives that value as the result. For example, the operation giving the maximum value of two values is idempotent: ma = x.
- Given a binary operation, an idempotent element for the operation is a value for which the operation, when given that value for both of its operands, gives the value as the result. For example, the number 1 is an idempotent of multiplication: 1 × 1 = 1.

A unary operation f that is a map from some set S into itself is called idempotent if, for all x in S,

f

In particular, the identity function id_S, defined by
id_S, is idempotent, as is the constant function K_c, where c is an element of S, defined by $K_c(x) = c$.

a. Absorption law
b. Idempotence
c. Antiisomorphism
d. Ordered exponential

9. In mathematics, _____ is a property that a binary operation can have. It means that, within an expression containing two or more of the same associative operators in a row, the order that the operations are performed does not matter as long as the sequence of the operands is not changed. That is, rearranging the parentheses in such an expression will not change its value.
a. Algebraically closed
b. Idempotence
c. Unital
d. Associativity

10. In mathematics, and in particular in abstract algebra, distributivity is a property of binary operations that generalises the _____ law from elementary algebra.
a. Closure with a twist
b. Distributive
c. Permutation
d. General linear group

11. In mathematics, a _____ is a convincing demonstration that some mathematical statement is necessarily true. _____s are obtained from deductive reasoning, rather than from inductive or empirical arguments. That is, a _____ must demonstrate that a statement is true in all cases, without a single exception.
a. Conchoid
b. Proof
c. Congruent
d. Germ

12. In propositional logic, contraposition is a logical relationship between two statements of material implication. A proposition Q is materially implicated by a proposition P when the following relationship holds:

$$(P \rightarrow Q)$$

In vernacular terms, this states 'If P then Q', or, 'If Socrates is a man then Socrates is human.' In a conditional such as this, P is called the antecedent and Q the consequent. One statement is the _____ of the other just when its antecedent is the negated consequent of the other, and vice-versa.

   a. Contrapositive
   b. Continuous signal
   c. Contour map
   d. Control chart

13. In mathematics, the _____ of a number n is the number that, when added to n, yields zero. The _____ of n is denoted −n. For example, 7 is −7, because 7 + (−7) = 0, and the _____ of −0.3 is 0.3, because −0.3 + 0.3 = 0.
   a. Algebraic structure
   b. Additive inverse
   c. Associativity
   d. Arity

14. In mathematics and logic, a _____ is a way of showing the truth or falsehood of a given statement by a straightforward combination of established facts, usually existing lemmas and theorems, without making any further assumptions. In order to directly prove a conditional statement of the form 'If p, then q', it is only necessary to consider situations where the statement p is true. Logical deduction is employed to reason from assumptions to conclusion.
   a. Minimal counterexample
   b. Proof by exhaustion
   c. Proofs from THE BOOK
   d. Direct proof

15. A hypothesis consists either of a suggested explanation for an observable phenomenon or of a reasoned proposal predicting a possible causal correlation among multiple phenomena. The term derives from the Greek, hypotithenai meaning 'to put under' or 'to suppose.' The scientific method requires that one can test a scientific hypothesis. Scientists generally base such _____ on previous observations or on extensions of scientific theories.

Chapter 11. LOGIC

a. 1-center problem
b. 2-3 heap
c. 120-cell
d. Hypotheses

16. In mathematics, the _____ is an approach to finding a particular solution to certain inhomogeneous ordinary differential equations and recurrence relations. It is closely related to the annihilator method, but instead of using a particular kind of differential operator in order to find the best possible form of the particular solution, a 'guess' is made as to the appropriate form, which is then tested by differentiating the resulting equation. In this sense, the _____ is less formal but more intuitive than the annihilator method.

a. Phase line
b. Linear differential equation
c. Method of undetermined coefficients
d. Differential algebraic equations

17. _____ is a branch of mathematics which focuses on the study of matrices. Initially a sub-branch of linear algebra, it has grown to cover subjects related to graph theory, algebra, combinatorics, and statistics as well.

The term matrix was first coined in 1848 by J.J. Sylvester as a name of an array of numbers.

a. Segre classification
b. Matrix theory
c. Semi-simple operators
d. Pairing

18. The Sheffer stroke, written '|' or '↑', in the subject matter of boolean functions or propositional calculus, denotes a logical operation that is equivalent to the negation of the conjunction operation, expressed in ordinary language as 'not both'. It is also called the alternative denial, since it says in effect that at least one of its operands is false. In Boolean algebra and digital electronics it is known as the _____ operation.

a. Recursion theory
b. NAND
c. Distribution rule
d. First-order logic

19. In mathematics, an _____ or member of a set is any one of the distinct objects that make up that set.

Writing A = {1,2,3,4}, means that the _____ s of the set A are the numbers 1, 2, 3 and 4. Groups of _____ s of A, for example {1,2}, are subsets of A.

a. Element
b. Order
c. Ideal
d. Universal code

20. In mathematics, and more specifically set theory, the _____ is the unique set having no members. Some axiomatic set theories assure that the _____ exists by including an axiom of _____; in other theories, its existence can be deduced. Many possible properties of sets are trivially true for the _____.
   a. A Mathematical Theory of Communication
   b. Empty set
   c. Inverse function
   d. Empty function

21. In mathematics, a _____ is a set that is negligible in some sense. For different applications, the meaning of 'negligible' varies. In measure theory, any set of measure 0 is called a _____.
   a. Prevalence and shyness
   b. Radonifying function
   c. Borel-Cantelli lemma
   d. Null set

22. In mathematics, especially in set theory, a set A is a _____ of a set B if A is 'contained' inside B. Notice that A and B may coincide. The relationship of one set being a _____ of another is called inclusion.
   a. Cartesian product
   b. Horizontal line test
   c. Set of all sets
   d. Subset

23. In mathematics, a _____ can mean either an element of the set {1, 2, 3, ...} or an element of the set {0, 1, 2, 3, ...}. The latter is especially preferred in mathematical logic, set theory, and computer science.

   _____s have two main purposes: they can be used for counting, and they can be used for ordering.

   a. Strong partition cardinal
   b. Suslin cardinal
   c. Cardinal numbers
   d. Natural number

24. The _____ are the set of numbers consisting of the natural numbers including 0 and their negatives. They are numbers that can be written without a fractional or decimal component, and fall within the set {... −2, −1, 0, 1, 2, ...}.

   a. A chemical equation
   b. A posteriori
   c. A Mathematical Theory of Communication
   d. Integers

25. In mathematics, a _____ is a number which can be expressed as a ratio of two integers. Non-integer _____s are usually written as the vulgar fraction $\frac{a}{b}$, where b is not zero. a is called the numerator, and b the denominator.

   a. Pre-algebra
   b. Tally marks
   c. Rational number
   d. Minkowski distance

26. In mathematics, a _____ can mean either an element of the set {1, 2, 3, ...} (i.e the positive integers) or an element of the set {0, 1, 2, 3, ...} (i.e. the non-negative integers).

   a. Whole number
   b. Bounded
   c. FISH
   d. Degrees of freedom

27. In mathematics, the _____s may be described informally in several different ways. The _____s include both rational numbers, such as 42 and −23/129, and irrational numbers, such as pi and the square root of two; or, a _____ can be given by an infinite decimal representation, such as 2.4871773339...., where the digits continue in some way; or, the _____s may be thought of as points on an infinitely long number line.

These descriptions of the _____s, while intuitively accessible, are not sufficiently rigorous for the purposes of pure mathematics.

   a. Tally marks
   b. Real number
   c. Minkowski distance
   d. Pre-algebra

28. _____ involves reducing the number of significant digits in a number. The result of _____ is a 'shorter' number having fewer non-zero digits yet similar in magnitude. The result is less precise but easier to use.

a. Rounding
b. Hyper operator
c. Shabakh
d. Sudan function

29. In statistics, _____ results in values that are limited above or below, similar to but distinct from the concept of statistical censoring.

Usually the values that insurance adjusters receive are either left-truncated, right-censored or both. For example, if policyholders are subject to a policy limit u, then any loss amounts that are actually above u are reported to the insurance company as being exactly u because u is the amount the insurance companies pay.

a. Descriptive research
b. Numerical analysis
c. Fixed point iteration
d. Truncation

30. In mathematics, a _____ is a rectangular table of elements, which may be numbers or, more generally, any abstract quantities that can be added and multiplied. Matrices are used to describe linear equations, keep track of the coefficients of linear transformations and to record data that depend on multiple parameters. Matrices are described by the field of _____ theory.
a. Double counting
b. Compression
c. Matrix
d. Coherent

31. _____ is the mathematical operation of scaling one number by another. It is one of the four basic operations in elementary arithmetic.

_____ is defined for whole numbers in terms of repeated addition; for example, 4 multiplied by 3 can be calculated by adding 3 copies of 4 together:

$$4 + 4 + 4 = 12.$$

_____ of rational numbers and real numbers is defined by systematic generalization of this basic idea.

a. The number 0 is even.
b. Least common multiple
c. Multiplication
d. Highest common factor

32. In mathematics, a _____ is the end result of a division problem. It can also be expressed as the number of times the divisor divides into the dividend.
   a. Marginal cost
   b. Quotient
   c. Notation
   d. Limiting

33. A _____ is a device for performing mathematical calculations, distinguished from a computer by having a limited problem solving ability and an interface optimized for interactive calculation rather than programming. _____s can be hardware or software, and mechanical or electronic, and are often built into devices such as PDAs or mobile phones.

Modern electronic _____s are generally small, digital, and usually inexpensive.

   a. 120-cell
   b. 1-center problem
   c. 2-3 heap
   d. Calculator

34. In mathematics, an _____ in the sense of ring theory is a subring $\mathcal{O}$ of a ring R that satisfies the conditions

   1. R is a ring which is a finite-dimensional algebra over the rational number field $\mathbb{Q}$
   2. $\mathcal{O}$ spans R over $\mathbb{Q}$, so that $\mathbb{Q}\mathcal{O} = R$, and
   3. $\mathcal{O}$ is a lattice in R.

The third condition can be stated more accurately, in terms of the extension of scalars of R to the real numbers, embedding R in a real vector space. In less formal terms, additively $\mathcal{O}$ should be a free abelian group generated by a basis for R over $\mathbb{Q}$.

The leading example is the case where R is a number field K and $\mathcal{O}$ is its ring of integers. In algebraic number theory there are examples for any K other than the rational field of proper subrings of the ring of integers that are also _____s.

a. Annihilator
b. Efficiency
c. Order
d. Algebraic

35. In algebra and computer programming, when a number or expression is both preceded and followed by a binary operation, a rule is required for which operation should be applied first; this rule is known as an _____ . From the earliest use of mathematical notation, multiplication took precedence over addition, whichever side of a number it appeared on. Thus 3 + 4 × 5 = 5 × 4 + 3 = 23.

a. Isomorphism class
b. Identity element
c. Order of operations
d. Algebraic K-theory

36. In functional analysis, a Banach space is called _____ if it satisfies a certain abstract property involving dual spaces. _____ spaces turn out to have desirable geometric properties.

Suppose X is a normed vector space over R or C.

a. Copula
b. Boolean algebra
c. Reflexive
d. Gamma test

37. In mathematics, the term _____ has several different important meanings:

- An _____ is an equality that remains true regardless of the values of any variables that appear within it, to distinguish it from an equality which is true under more particular conditions. For this, the 'triple bar' symbol ≡ is sometimes used.
- In algebra, an _____ or _____ element of a set S with a binary operation Â· is an element e that, when combined with any element x of S, produces that same x. That is, eÂ·x = xÂ·e = x for all x in S.
  - The _____ function from a set S to itself, often denoted id or id_S, s the function such that i = x for all x in S. This function serves as the _____ element in the set of all functions from S to itself with respect to function composition.
  - In linear algebra, the _____ matrix of size n is the n-by-n square matrix with ones on the main diagonal and zeros elsewhere. This matrix serves as the _____ with respect to matrix multiplication.

A common example of the first meaning is the trigonometric _____

$$\sin^2 \theta + \cos^2 \theta = 1$$

which is true for all real values of θ, as opposed to

$$\cos \theta = 1,$$

which is true only for some values of θ, not all. For example, the latter equation is true when $\theta = 0$, false when $\theta = 2$

The concepts of 'additive _____' and 'multiplicative _____' are central to the Peano axioms. The number 0 is the 'additive _____' for integers, real numbers, and complex numbers. For the real numbers, for all $a \in \mathbb{R}$,

$$0 + a = a,$$

$a + 0 = a$, and

$$0 + 0 = 0.$$

Similarly, The number 1 is the 'multiplicative _____' for integers, real numbers, and complex numbers.

a. Action
b. Identity
c. ARIA
d. Intersection

38. In mathematics, a _____ for a number x, denoted by $\frac{1}{x}$ or x^{-1}, is a number which when multiplied by x yields the multiplicative identity, 1. The _____ of x is also called the reciprocal of x. The _____ of a fraction p/q is q/p.
a. Golden function
b. Hyperbolic function
c. Double exponential
d. Multiplicative inverse

39. In mathematics, the multiplicative inverse of a number x, denoted 1/x or x^{-1}, is the number which, when multiplied by x, yields 1. The multiplicative inverse of x is also called the _____ of x.

a. 2-3 heap
b. 1-center problem
c. Reciprocal
d. 120-cell

40. In the mathematical areas of algebra and analysis, the _____, is an abstract and explicit statement of the familiar property from elementary mathematics that if the product of two real numbers is zero, then at least one of the numbers in the product (factors) must be zero.
a. Distributive
b. Zero-product property
c. Group extension
d. Hyperstructures

41. In arithmetic and number theory, the _____ or lowest common multiple or smallest common multiple of two integers a and b is the smallest positive integer that is a multiple of both a and b. Since it is a multiple, it can be divided by a and b without a remainder. If either a or b is 0, so that there is no such positive integer, then lc is defined to be zero.
a. Least common multiple
b. Plus-minus sign
c. Lowest common denominator
d. Plus and minus signs

42. In mathematics, a _____ is a picture of a straight line in which the integers are shown as specially-marked points evenly spaced on the line. Although this image only shows the integers from -9 to 9, the line includes all real numbers, continuing 'forever' in each direction. It is often used as an aid in teaching simple addition and subtraction, especially involving negative numbers.
a. Number line
b. Real number
c. Number system
d. Point plotting

43. In mathematics, the _____ of a Euclidean space is a special point, usually denoted by the letter O, used as a fixed point of reference for the geometry of the surrounding space. In a Cartesian coordinate system, the _____ is the point where the axes of the system intersect. In Euclidean geometry, the _____ may be chosen freely as any convenient point of reference.

Chapter 11. LOGIC

   a. OMAC
   b. Autonomous system
   c. Interval
   d. Origin

44. In mathematics, an _____ is a statement about the relative size or order of two objects, or about whether they are the same or not

- The notation a < b means that a is less than b.
- The notation a > b means that a is greater than b.
- The notation a ≠ b means that a is not equal to b, but does not say that one is bigger than the other or even that they can be compared in size.

In all these cases, a is not equal to b, hence, '_____'.

These relations are known as strict _____

- The notation a ≤ b means that a is less than or equal to b;
- The notation a ≥ b means that a is greater than or equal to b;

An additional use of the notation is to show that one quantity is much greater than another, normally by several orders of magnitude.

- The notation a << b means that a is much less than b.
- The notation a >> b means that a is much greater than b.

If the sense of the _____ is the same for all values of the variables for which its members are defined, then the _____ is called an 'absolute' or 'unconditional' _____. If the sense of an _____ holds only for certain values of the variables involved, but is reversed or destroyed for other values of the variables, it is called a conditional _____.

An _____ may appear unsolvable because it only states whether a number is larger or smaller than another number; but it is possible to apply the same operations for equalities to inequalities. For example, to find x for the _____ 10x > 23 one would divide 23 by 10.

   a. Inequality
   b. A posteriori
   c. A Mathematical Theory of Communication
   d. A chemical equation

Chapter 11. LOGIC

45. In mathematical writing, the adjective _____ is used to modify technical terms which have multiple meanings. It indicates that the exclusive meaning of the term is to be understood. (More formally, one could say that this is the meaning which implies the other meanings.)

   a. Percentage points
   b. Jargon
   c. Strict
   d. Well-behaved

46. In mathematics, the _____ of a real number is its numerical value without regard to its sign. So, for example, 3 is the _____ of both 3 and −3.

The _____ of a number a is denoted by $|a|$.

Generalizations of the _____ for real numbers occur in a wide variety of mathematical settings.

   a. Area hyperbolic functions
   b. Absolute value
   c. A chemical equation
   d. A Mathematical Theory of Communication

47. In abstract algebra, a field extension L /K is called _____ if every element of L is _____ over K. Field extensions which are not _____.

For example, the field extension R/Q, that is the field of real numbers as an extension of the field of rational numbers, is transcendental, while the field extensions C/R and Q

   a. Identity
   b. Algebraic
   c. Ideal
   d. Echo

48. In mathematics, especially in the area of abstract algebra known as ring theory, a _____ is a ring with 0 ≠ 1 such that ab = 0 implies that either a = 0 or b = 0. That is, it is a nontrivial ring without left or right zero divisors. A commutative _____ is called an integral _____.

   a. Left primitive ring
   b. Simple ring
   c. Modular representation theory
   d. Domain

Chapter 11. LOGIC

49. In the study of metric spaces in mathematics, there are various notions of two metrics on the same underlying space being 'the same', or _____.

In the following, M will denote a non-empty set and d_1 and d_2 will denote two metrics on M.

The two metrics d_1 and d_2 are said to be topologically _____ if they generate the same topology on M.

   a. Equivalent
   b. A Mathematical Theory of Communication
   c. A posteriori
   d. A chemical equation

50. In mathematics and computer science, _____ (also base-16, hexa or base, of 16. It uses sixteen distinct symbols, most often the symbols 0-9 to represent values zero to nine, and A, B, C, D, E, F (or a through f) to represent values ten to fifteen.

Its primary use is as a human friendly representation of binary coded values, so it is often used in digital electronics and computer engineering.

   a. Hexadecimal
   b. Radix
   c. Tetradecimal
   d. Factoradic

51. Exponentiation is a mathematical operation, written a^n, involving two numbers, the base a and the _____ n. When n is a positive integer, exponentiation corresponds to repeated multiplication:

$$a^n = \underbrace{a \times \cdots \times a}_{n},$$

just as multiplication by a positive integer corresponds to repeated addition:

$$a \times n = \underbrace{a + \cdots + a}_{n}.$$

The _____ is usually shown as a superscript to the right of the base. The exponentiation a^n can be read as: a raised to the n-th power, a raised to the power [of] n or possibly a raised to the _____ [of] n, or more briefly: a to the n-th power or a to the power [of] n, or even more briefly: a to the n.

a. Exponentiating by squaring
b. Exponent
c. Exponential sum
d. Exponential tree

52. In vascular plants, the _____ is the organ of a plant body that typically lies below the surface of the soil. This is not always the case, however, since a _____ can also be aerial (that is, growing above the ground) or aerating (that is, growing up above the ground or especially above water.) Furthermore, a stem normally occurring below ground is not exceptional either

a. 2-3 heap
b. 120-cell
c. 1-center problem
d. Root

53. In mathematics, the _____ of a number to a given base is the power or exponent to which the base must be raised in order to produce the number.

For example, the _____ of 1000 to the base 10 is 3, because 3 is how many 10s one must multiply to get 1000: thus 10 × 10 × 10 = 1000; the base-2 _____ of 32 is 5 because 5 is how many 2s one must multiply to get 32: thus 2 × 2 × 2 × 2 × 2 = 32. In the language of exponents: $10^3 = 1000$, so $\log_{10} 1000 = 3$, and $2^5 = 32$, so $\log_2 32 = 5$.

a. 120-cell
b. 2-3 heap
c. 1-center problem
d. Logarithm

54. In mathematics and in the sciences, a _____ (plural: _____e, formulæ or _____s) is a concise way of expressing information symbolically (as in a mathematical or chemical _____), or a general relationship between quantities. One of many famous _____e is Albert Einstein's $E = mc^2$ (see special relativity

In mathematics, a _____ is a key to solve an equation with variables. For example, the problem of determining the volume of a sphere is one that requires a significant amount of integral calculus to solve.

a. 2-3 heap
b. 120-cell
c. 1-center problem
d. Formula

55. In mathematics, _____ and undefined are used to explain whether or not expressions have meaningful, sensible, and unambiguous values. Not all branches of mathematics come to the same conclusion.

The following expressions are undefined in all contexts, but remarks in the analysis section may apply.

a. Defined
b. LHS
c. Plugging in
d. Toy model

56. Leonardo of Pisa (c. 1170 - c. 1250), also known as Leonardo Pisano, Leonardo Bonacci, Leonardo _____, or, most commonly, simply _____, was an Italian mathematician, considered by some 'the most talented mathematician of the Middle Ages'.
a. Fibonacci
b. Guido Castelnuovo
c. Harry Hinsley
d. Ralph C. Merkle

57. In geometry, a _____ is defined as a quadrilateral where all four of its angles are right angles.
a. Polytope
b. Point group in two dimensions
c. Cantor-Dedekind axiom
d. Rectangle

58. A _____ is an opening in a wall that allows the passage of light and, if not closed or sealed, air and sound. _____s are usually glazed or covered in some other transparent or translucent material. _____s are held in place by frames, which prevent them from collapsing in.
a. 120-cell
b. 1-center problem
c. 2-3 heap
d. Window

ANSWER KEY

Chapter 1
1. c   2. d   3. b   4. b   5. c   6. b   7. a   8. c   9. b   10. d
11. d   12. c   13. c   14. d   15. d   16. d   17. a   18. d   19. c   20. b
21. d   22. a   23. d   24. d   25. d   26. a   27. b   28. d   29. d   30. d
31. d   32. c   33. a   34. c   35. c   36. d   37. d   38. d   39. d   40. a
41. a

Chapter 2
1. d   2. b   3. b   4. c   5. d   6. b   7. c   8. d   9. d   10. d
11. c   12. b   13. b   14. d   15. d   16. a   17. b   18. d   19. b   20. b
21. c   22. d   23. d   24. d   25. d   26. c   27. a   28. d

Chapter 3
1. a   2. d   3. d   4. d   5. b   6. b   7. d   8. d   9. d

Chapter 4
1. d   2. d   3. b   4. a   5. b   6. a   7. a   8. a   9. b   10. d
11. d   12. a   13. d   14. d   15. b   16. d   17. a   18. b

Chapter 5
1. d   2. d   3. d   4. b   5. d   6. b   7. b   8. d   9. c

Chapter 6
1. d   2. a   3. d   4. d   5. d   6. d   7. a   8. b   9. b   10. d
11. d   12. d   13. d   14. d   15. a   16. a   17. a   18. c   19. d   20. d
21. b   22. d   23. d   24. c   25. d   26. d   27. a   28. d   29. c

Chapter 7
1. d   2. d   3. c   4. c   5. c   6. d   7. d   8. d   9. c   10. d
11. a   12. d   13. c   14. c   15. d   16. a   17. d   18. d   19. a

Chapter 8
1. d   2. d   3. b   4. d   5. d   6. d   7. d   8. d   9. b   10. b
11. b   12. d   13. d   14. d   15. d   16. b   17. b

Chapter 9
1. b   2. a   3. d   4. a   5. c   6. b   7. a   8. d   9. d   10. d
11. c   12. a   13. b   14. c   15. b   16. d   17. d   18. d   19. b   20. b
21. d   22. c   23. c   24. a   25. a   26. b   27. d   28. d   29. a   30. b
31. d   32. b   33. d   34. d   35. c   36. b   37. c   38. d   39. b   40. c
41. b   42. a   43. b

Chapter 10
1. d   2. a   3. d   4. d   5. d   6. d   7. d   8. a   9. b   10. d
11. d   12. c   13. d   14. d   15. d   16. b   17. c   18. b   19. b

ANSWER KEY

Chapter 11

1. a	2. d	3. d	4. d	5. b	6. c	7. b	8. b	9. d	10. b
11. b	12. a	13. b	14. d	15. d	16. c	17. b	18. b	19. a	20. b
21. d	22. d	23. d	24. d	25. c	26. a	27. b	28. a	29. d	30. c
31. c	32. b	33. d	34. c	35. c	36. c	37. b	38. d	39. c	40. b
41. a	42. a	43. d	44. a	45. c	46. b	47. b	48. d	49. a	50. a
51. b	52. d	53. d	54. d	55. a	56. a	57. d	58. d		

www.ingramcontent.com/pod-product-compliance
Lightning Source LLC
Chambersburg PA
CBHW081844230426
43669CB00018B/2818